Writing and Publishing Personal Essays

Sheila Bender

Silver Threads
San Diego, California

Writing and Publishing Personal Essays

For information, contact Silver Threads, 3830 Valley Center Drive, #705, PMB 102, San Diego, California 92130 (858-794-1597)

Silver Threads is an imprint of Silvercat™

ISBN 1-93067-05-X

Distributed to the trade by Book Clearing House, 800-431-1579, www.bookch.com

Publisher's Cataloging in Publication Data

Bender, Sheila.

    Writing and publishing personal essays / Sheila Bender. — 1st ed. — San Diego, Calif. : Silver Threads, 2005.

      p. ; cm.

    Includes bibliographical references.
    ISBN 1-893067-05-X

    1. Essay—Authorship. 2. Autobiography—Authorship. 3. English language—Rhetoric. 4. Authorship—Marketing. I. Title.

PE1479.A88 B46 2005
808/.042—dc22   0502

printed in the United States of America

For my mother,
Arline Lillian,
who lets me know when my writing touches her,

and for my dad,
Bert Lillian,
who would definitely have been tickled to see this book.

People are hungry,
and one good word is bread
for a thousand.

—From "Loaves and Fishes"
by David Whyte

Contents

Acknowledgements

I want to thank Bob Goodman for his unwavering support in keeping my instruction on writing essays out in book form, my husband Kurt VanderSluis for his help as always in constructive editing and all my writer friends and colleagues who have contributed essays to this book as models for others who long to share their experience.

Credits

"Let Your Writer Self Be With You" by Sheila Bender appeared in *Writing It Real* on September 14, 2002.

"A Close Call" by James Bertolino appeared in *Goat-Footed Turtle*, Stone Marrow Press, Guemes Island, WA 1996.

"Feast of All Souls," by Susan Bono appeared in *Tiny Lights: A Journal of Personal Essay,* Vol. 8, No. 2.

"Baby Lust" by Janice Eidus appeared in *110 Stories: New York Writes After September 11,* New York University Press, 2002.

"Softball" by Susan Hagen appeared in *Tiny Lights: A Journal of Personal Essay,* Vol. 5, No. 2.

"The View from in Here: What Attention Deficit Disorder Feels Like)" by Janis Jaquith is excerpted from her book of collected essays, *Birdseed Cookies: A Fractured Memoir,* Xlibris Corporation, 2001.

"Adoptions Not Always the Stuff of Fairy Tales" by Christi Killien appeared in the *Seattle Post-Intelligencer,* November 16, 2002.

"The Lighted Lamp of Emma Lazarus" by Nancy Smiler Levinson appeared in the *The Los Angeles Times* in 1986.

"The Accidental Student" by Susan Luzader appeared in the December 2001 issue of *The Desert Leaf,* Tucson, AZ.

"The Locker Room" by Roy Nims appeared in the 1995 edition of *Writing Personal Essays: How to Shape Your Life Experiences for the Page.*

"Eating Pizza With Stacy," by Bora Lee Reed appeared in *Tiny Lights: A Journal of Personal Essay,* Vol. 9, No. 1.

"Why Cats Write" by Joanne Rocklin first appeared in the May, 1996 issue of *The Bulletin,* the newsletter of the Society of Children's Book Writers and Illustrators.

"Dreams of Going" by Barbara Stahura appeared in the Midwest *Women's Forum* in June 1994 and is also online at http://www.wordjourneys.com/dreamgo.htm.

"After the Ball" by Steven Winn appeared under the headline "Good Day at the Ballpark Turns Great in the Retelling" in the June 16, 2002 *San Francisco Chronicle.*

On Shaping Life Experiences for the Page

I fell in love with the essay form when I began teaching freshman English at community colleges in the Seattle area. I had just finished my graduate studies in creative writing, where I had worked for several years with acclaimed poets and learned a process for generating poetry and revising it that allowed me to speak clearly, movingly and forcefully from my deepest self. I had also learned how to coach others in writing their poems more fully and completely.

But as gratifying as working on poems was, it didn't pay the bills, and so like many others in my class, I sought work teaching freshman composition, a course our Masters degrees in writing qualified us to teach. Once in the classroom, I realized I could share what I'd learned from poets with my composition students, who were struggling to get their ideas and experience on the page.

In school, I had learned how to farm experience for insight and how to work past the droughts and floods that threatened the coveted crop of poems. Now reading professional essays from anthologies and reading the life experience of my students in their essay drafts, I realized that I resonated with this prose, as I did with poetry, and that the best of the finished student and professional essays worked as lyrically as poems do. They used sound and rhythm, cadence, repetition, images, and pattern to retrieve experience and make discoveries. When they succeeded, these essays picked the reader up, took the reader on a journey, and placed the reader back on the ground again, stunned but clear-headed, as poems do. I was helping diverse individuals—a young diabetic who was writing about what being a diabetic means to a younger patient (denial and rebellion), a divorced single mom who was raising a bi-racial child, and a contractor with twenty-years' job experience find words to express his belief in the miraculous. I loved my work. I loved my students and their essays, and I loved the published ones I read with them.

Over the next fourteen years, I developed a curriculum for writing essays based on combining patterns of thinking with the sensitivities of the poet. I published my approach in the 1995 edition of *Writing Personal Essays: How to Shape YourLife Experience for the Page.* In the years since I published that book, I have coached hundreds of people on their way to fully writing essays they didn't realize they had in them. Wanting to offer my students and readers more exercises for mining their ideas and more ways to craft essays, I set to work on articles for *Writer's Digest Magazine.* Next, I began an online instructional magazine, *Writing It Real* at www.writingitreal.com for those who write from personal experience. Because essays have a strong place in today's publications and among today's audiences, I am excited to offer this updated and extended edition, *Writing and Publishing Personal Essays,* containing new sample essays, new instructional material, and new marketing information that will work whether you have already published many essays or are just now looking into finding homes for them.

Your joy in writing personal essays will come from the surprises you encounter in writing them. As Robert Atwan writes in his introduction to *The Best American Essays, 2001,* "Surprise . . . keeps 'life writing' live writing." My instruction is dedicated to helping you find surprise in your thoughts and keep the surprise alive in your writing; it is dedicated to helping you grow essays instead of tearing them apart with criticism. Beginning drafts are much like cotyledons—the first leaves on a plant that store nutrition for the shapely leaves and flowers that come next. When the signature shape is there, the cotyledons fall away; so it is with writing. The parts of essay drafts no longer necessary in the writing's final form fall away, too.

In the chapters ahead, I will show you how to work the fertile soil of your experience, seed your essays, grow your essays, and prepare them for market. I intend this book as a "growers guide" to success.

Prologue to the First Edition

At 45

Note: I am a decade older than when I wrote this essay for the 1995 edition of my book, but everything I realized remains important.

The way I see it, I am at the halfway mark in my life, more or less. Writing this sentence, I suddenly remember my pre-teen self as I cut through the aquamarine water on swimming race days summers at the Greenwood Swim Club in East Hanover, New Jersey. Mid-way down the lane and desperate to take a breath, I'd struggle to keep myself from looking around as I opened my mouth for a quick gulp of air. My head back in the water, I'd look to my left and to my right. How far had I come? Were any swimmers behind me in their lanes? How many?

Waiting to hear the names of the winners, I'd stand with the other girls, panting and dripping, self-conscious about the way my ribs and navel showed between the two pieces of my bathing suit. I wasn't exactly a fish in the water, as my parents and their friends would describe other children, but I wanted to be a part of things. I wore the right bathing suit, swam the crawl stroke races, learned to dive from the high dive, and danced with the teenyboppers to rock and roll from the clubhouse jukebox.

I worked so hard to look like the kind of fish everyone else seemed to be that I didn't know what it felt like to be the kind of fish I actually was. All of my growing up, I felt like a hypocrite, a working-hard-to-be-a-part-of-things person on the outside covering up for a sidelines kind of a girl on the inside. Though I wanted to be sponsored to live on an Indian reservation one summer, I stayed home and enrolled in the short hand course my mother wanted me to take. Though I longed to go out with our high school's gawky first chair violinist who enjoyed long walks more than school dances, I dated the president of our youth group. Though the only science facts I could remember vividly were ones like "when you smell manure, you are actually taking particles of the substance into your nose," I declared I would be a science major on my college applications because all the smart kids were going into science. Though I longed to travel and live abroad, I finished college and became a teacher so I had a career I could fall back on, something my mother told me time and again was necessary. She wanted me to have a career that would wait for me when I had children. To have children, I married a guy who was swimming in the same water I was trying so hard to stay in.

While he was in medical school, I directed a day care center. When he became an intern and we had kids, I asked for a leave from my job. I sat in the bleachers during my kids' swimming lesson days discussing Volvos and home furnishings with the parents beside me. I chauffeured and shepherded my kids from class to class, playmate's house to playmate's house, pre-school potluck to pre-school potluck. I was a good wife to my tired and overworked husband. I ran off one evening a week to take a watercolor class at the community center and one day a week to volunteer at the juvenile court. It seemed all right from the outside, but raising my children was rapidly becoming the first job I couldn't succeed at with sheer activity. I loved them too deeply. I knew at my core my hypocrite days were over. Raising them to be happy would mean raising them to be the true people they were inside. How could I do that if I denied them who I was? I would have to shed that person working so hard at swimming to the end of the lane and find the person who was lurking on the sidelines. What was her element?

Folding the unending piles of laundry in my life, I began to hear poetic lines inside my head. I had only written in grade school and then once or twice when I was in high school. But poetry books by people I'd never heard of had jumped of their own accord into my hands since college whenever I visited bookstores. I never spoke of this to anybody, but I had taken to buying them; the books insisted on it. Now that I was hearing these lines, I started to write stanzas during my children's naptime. I felt like a song was there in the sounds I was making, but the words didn't convey much. I had found the tune my inner self sang, but I didn't know the words to it. I continued reading poems voraciously and trying to write them.

The next summer, when I was looking for classes for my children, I found a catalog from the University of Washington, and I read about poet David Wagoner's Poetry Writing Workshop. I would need to submit poems to be considered for the workshop, so I struggled to rework the few "almost poems" I had managed to pull from myself all those nap times.

The day I was to drop them off at the Creative Writing Office, a good friend and I headed to the campus with our strollers and diaper bags and my envelope of poems.

"Why aren't I applying to social work school?" I lamented. "Then people would believe I was going to help others when I got my graduate degree, not sit around finding out my thoughts and feelings."

My friend assured me writing poetry was a humanitarian act.

"Right," I said, "but I really can't shake the idea that I am supposed to do something to serve my country. To be a good citizen."

"It's that Sputnik thing again, isn't it?"

I nodded. When the Russians successfully launched Sputnik, I saw my grade school teachers cry telling us students that our country was now at risk. All classes reported to the auditorium where we were told how important physical fitness, science, and math were to be from then on and how art and music were not as important in our battle to regain leadership of the world.

"I had a lot of trouble climbing the thick hairy ropes they suddenly hung from the gym ceiling, but I thought I could help another way. I feel guilty about poetry. People think it's superfluous and dilettantish," I said.

"Learning your own heart is a big contribution," my wise friend said. "Do know how much better the world would be if more people had true insight?"

Amazingly, David Wagoner accepted me into his class. In September, I began going to that class three times a week. No matter how hard it was to make child care arrangements or how much trouble I had parking or how many times my poems were heavily criticized or how many times not one student in the class seemed to care what I said since I was new and unpublished, I was happy. David Wagoner's class was the first place I had ever congregated where I was completely at peace. I understood the thinking and the ideas. I liked what we talked about and I liked what we did. I knew I would learn how to do it better. It didn't matter if anyone else recognized this about me. It was enough that I recognized it. My classmates could tear into my poems and I never flinched. In class, I never felt time go by. I was never out of breath. I didn't think about who might be ahead of me. It didn't matter how far I had come to get there or how far I would need to go.

As my children grew, I wrote and learned and published. To get a poem to both sound right and mean right, I had to listen closely to it, check it with my ear and with my heart, until all my conscious mind's attempts to short circuit the revelation of truths or supply unearned truths were stopped. Each time I wrote, I had to get beyond what my "good girl-good citizen" self propounded and find the sources of pain and joy in my life, no matter how small or how large, how alike they were to those of others or how different they seemed. My conversations with my children became passage-ways into my poems. When my daughter told me that when she grew up, I would grow down, I wrote about that, and I shared what I wrote with her. Though she may not have understood the meaning of my words, she learned the sound of her mother's heart and mind. When she told me she dreamed I came out of the sky with the raindrops and opened my umbrella and floated back down to earth watering the flowers, I felt more real than I ever had winning a race or getting a job.

Poetry had taken me to my inner self. Everything I had accu-mulated with my old outer self fell away, including my marriage. The hardest thing about saying goodbye to my marriage was being unable to explain to my parents and relatives why I was doing it. They had never seen the inside me. They didn't really trust insides or foster recognizing them. They said my divorce was making them sick. The fact that I couldn't be heard no matter what I said allowed me to give up trying. I wasn't going to swim in the wrong element for myself anymore. My children understood me without much explanation. My son would fall asleep nights to the sound of my Olivetti truck of an electric typewriter and report to people that the only problem with having a poet for a mom was hearing the typewriter at night. I became a teacher of writing at commu-nity centers and community colleges, a state artist-in-residence, and a member of literary project boards. When I was over-whelmed with other people's writing and the administrative details of the projects, my son told me he wanted to build me a house on wheels so he could drive me around and I could be free to write and write.

I am remarried now to a man who found me through my poems. He was a friend of one of my best friends when my first book of poems, a locally published 20-page chapbook, came out.

He saw it on her coffee table, and he read it while she was on the telephone. Then he asked her how she had found this poet. When she said I was her friend, he insisted on organizing a picnic to meet my children and me. That was almost ten years ago.

There have been many eddies and stagnant pools in the new waters of my life, but always the flow of fresh water, which poetry brings, has cleared me of those spots. This week I am turning 45. As my last child prepares to leave the nest this summer, a proposal for my third book is in my agent's enthusiastic hands.

I know how far I have come. I enjoy recognizing myself as someone who has let her true self emerge, who won't need to push herself down the wrong lane anymore, desperate for breath. I think often of my grandfather in summer, the way he floated on his back in the Atlantic Ocean off Coney Island, hands behind his head for a pillow. He was the only person I knew who could float as long as he wanted to without sculling his hands or kicking his legs. There he is, smiling and buoyant, the water glistening with sun.

How to Use This Book

. . . the real possibility of the personal essay, which is to catch oneself in the act of being human . . . means a willingness to surrender for a time our pose of unshakable rectitude, and to admit that we are, despite our best intentions, subject to all manner of doubt and weakness and foolish wanting.

—Tobias Wolff

*I*n the introduction, I talk about growing essays, and I believe that farming is an accurate metaphor for the process of essay writing. But it is also useful to compare finished essays to vessels engineered according to their function and built from raw experience. Some personal essays turn out to be cruise ships, some battleships, some tugs, some sailboats and some simple dories, but all of them, when finished, take their authors and their readers across waters they might not otherwise have negotiated.

What is the guiding plan for making the vessel? What is the practice by which one shakes a pose of rectitude or even recognizes it? How does a personal essay tell its author's story intimately and with real meaning for others?

The age-old rhetorical styles of description, narration, how-to, comparison and contrast, classification and division, cause and effect, definition and argument and persuasion are crucial to building essays. When a writer begins writing with a particular question in mind and knows which style is best suited for exploring the answer, a shapely, insightful essay results. To help writers ensure that they will write shapely essays, I have developed eight "write questions," one for each style of rhetoric. These questions guarantee a writer can extract the particular life experience best explored by each style and with the help of each style's inherent structure, know how to put experience on the page for exploration and insight. To guarantee that writers create a rich piece of work, full of the details that build intimacy, I offer "gathering exercises" that help focus writers on their material, many elements of which may have been long buried. To this new edition of the book, I have added discussions of new sample essays in each style. These essays are written by people with a variety of personal experience and will help you form a sense of what your vessels will look like.

Whatever form your essay takes, using this methodology, you will create an intimate piece of writing. The word intimate is a word that is used as three different parts of speech: adjective, noun, and verb. If we apply it in all of its meanings, we will know the work of a personal essayist and essay: As an adjective, intimate means personal, private, detailed, deep, innermost. As a noun, it means close friend or associate. As a verb, it means to make known indirectly or to hint at. To tell your story intimately, you must attend to the personal, private details of your life. Then your essay becomes your close friend. The details in the essay hint at a deeper meaning; you follow them toward understanding what you didn't understand before you sat down to write.

Essayist Nancy Mairs uses a different metaphor in her book, *Ordinary Time*: "It's as though some writers have the sense never to enter the room until they've thrown the switch and flooded it with light, whereas others, like me, insist on entering rooms with burnt-out bulbs or blown fuses or maybe no wiring at all." When you write an essay, you set out on an exploration without knowing what was in the rooms or even which of your life's buildings you'll explore. I am convinced that the best learning and the best teaching take place that way. We don't always recognize what in our drafts is "on topic" and what is "another story." We don't always recognize where we have written "place holders" for deeper, richer material and where we have skated over lucrative emotional information and details. Finding these areas is an important part of the essay-writing process. I will share a response method that will help the readers you ask to identify such places, and your writing will get stronger and stronger.

When you come to essays as farmers, shipwrights, and inhabitants of home, to do a good job, you have to divide your work into steps. You must invent, then shape, and then, lastly, edit.

As you explore the eight "write" questions and rhetorical styles in this book, you will use specially focused invention exercises and the three-step response method for finding your material and shaping it. In Chapter XI, I include information on further shaping as well as editing. You will read about "deep listening" and "identifying occasion" as parts of the shaping process and about common punctuation, spelling and grammar errors to watch for. In Chapter XII, I review the process for submitting work for publication. In the book's Appendix, I provide useful resources for writers of personal essays, from Web sites, magazines and books to festivals and learning programs.

In each chapter, after you do exercises to mine material, reread the sample essays with an eye toward seeing how the authors might have intuitively done similar exercises that helped yield the details and images they needed for their essays. Two of the authors, Roy Nims and Timothy Johnson, were students in writing workshops at the time they wrote the essays reprinted in this book. The others have a publishing history. Whether the sample essays are by published or unpublished authors, they will prove instructive as they demonstrate the particular essay style each author put to use in crafting their experience for the page. As you work, you will see how much of the material you generate in exercises ends up in your finished essay.

One more note before we begin: Trust your experience, whatever it has been. Do not believe that only the extraordinary is worthy of writing and publishing. Believe instead that making the ordinary extraordinary is the work of the personal essayist. Robert Atwan, founding editor of the annual *Best American Essays* series from Houghton Mifflin, said in a 1995 interview in *Poets & Writer's Magazine*:

> Someone can go around the world and write a boring essay, and someone like Henry Thoreau could walk a mile in Concord and write a fascinating essay. What makes an essay of quality is thought and reflection.

Whether you want to use trekking in Nepal or walking to your corner grocery store as your subject, you have essays to write and much to learn from the process. Rainer Maria Rilke tells us in his famous *Letters to a Young Poet*:

> ... trust ... in the small Things that hardly anyone sees and that can so suddenly become huge, immeasurable; if you have this love for what is humble and try very simply, as someone who serves, to win the confidence of what seems poor: then everything will become easier for you, more coherent ... in your innermost awareness, awakeness, and knowledge ... [translated from the German by M.D. Herter Norton, WW. Norton, 1994 edition]

Writing the personal essay, like writing poetry, means renewing a contract with life; how can you even think of delaying getting started?

Chapter II

Empower Yourself to Write the Personal Essay

I believe that I am not alone in my attempts to create,
And that once I begin the work, settle into the strangeness,
The words will take shape, the form find life, and the spirit take flight.
                                   —Jan Phillips
                                   Marry Your Muse

We are writers. . . . The words became our friends and our companions,
and without even saying it aloud, a thought danced with them: I can do
this. This is who I am.
                                   —Anna Quindlen
                                   How Reading Changed My Life

*T*hrough the techniques of writing the personal essay, you can recall your experience and release the essence of it in fewer pages than you might imagine. You can write about the time you waited in the car while your father went into his mother's house to receive an "heirloom," came out empty handed and slammed the driver's side door so hard the car rocked like a boat in tall waves. You can write about the time you walked home from high school on a windy day and your mother told you to look at yourself in the mirror because you were so beautiful in the flush of early spring. You can write about the time the toaster oven you'd received as a wedding gift burnt out and you knew for certain this was a metaphor for your marriage. If you have ever found yourself saying, "If only I could write a book about my life" or "I want to write but I don't know exactly what I want to write," the personal essay is right for you, because you will be able to write to the essence of your experience and find out what it is you have to say.

The term essay may be lumped together in the files of your mind with the dreaded weekly theme and the boring what-I-did-over-my-school-vacation assignments of childhood. If writing was dull, difficult, and removed from anything you really felt, it might have been because you felt your life was not important enough to merit words on a page or because you "couldn't describe things in words" the way you experienced them in life. Perhaps you felt the teacher wanted to hear something other than what was true for you or perhaps you were afraid to put your truths on paper.

In Chapter I, I addressed the need for every author of personal essays to acknowledge the elements of their lives, no matter how mundane, in order to draw meaning from them. In following chapters, I will offer exercises to help you gather words for writing your experiences. Here, though, I would like to address two more inhibitors to good writing: fear of your audience and fear of your truths.

You have the right to say what you want to about your experience. It is, in fact, essential. Using the personal essay, you have what book reviewer Joan Frank describes in the July/August, 1990 *Utne Reader*:

> . . . a two-way mirror, prompting a startling moment wherein writer and reader each recognize some aspect of themselves in the other and come away from that moment transformed.

When you write a personal essay, you write on a topic of your choice, because you want to find the truth in your experience. If you find it, your essay will be interesting to someone else. You and your essay are in charge, not your high school or college English teacher. In fact, as you will find out in the following chapters, your essay itself will be your teacher. This teacher serves you, however, only when you trust in your vulnerability.

In a poem called "Moccasin Flowers," poet Mary Oliver, writes:

But all my life—so far—
I have loved best
how the flowers rise
and open, how

the pink lungs of their bodies
enter the fire of the world
and stand there shining
and willing . . .

I believe that words and images come to the person who stands "there shining and willing," that life's fire can provoke us into bringing forth our voices, rich with human qualities. As writers, we can take a lesson from the lodgepole pine, with its cones that open and drop seeds when fires scorch the forest floor. Let life's fire provoke you into bringing forth your voice, rich with human qualities.

Seek Knowledge through Writing

Getting to the flower of true voice requires work. Just as a seed cannot perform the miracle of growing into a new plant until it is released from what encloses it, often you must crack open the experience of your life to find the true seed from which to write. In doing so, you learn something new about yourself and your circumstances.

I may think I have a funny story to tell about the time my sister and I went to New Haven, Connecticut, to visit our great aunt and her two sons. I may think what is important is recounting every detail of that first train trip I took between Newark, N.J. and New Haven. Yet when I write, I remember the new hats my mother insisted we wear for the trip because "Aunt Bertha is from wealthy New England." I remember how we excitedly put the hats on as the train was pulling into the station. Greeting us, Aunt Bertha insisted we take the hats off immediately. "They look so silly," she said. When I write that and re-experience Aunt Bertha saying those words, I recognize that the deep experience of my train ride is not the ride itself but what it felt like to be a stranger.

How can you consistently get beyond mere recounting of experience and find the wisdom and knowing inside it? The eight "write" questions I share, along with exercises for answering them, will help you both think of personal experience topics and make discoveries in your writing. Using games, I will help you understand the pattern of thinking used in each essay form. By combining your understanding of the form with your answer to the "write" question, you will achieve essays that release your experience onto the page in compelling essays that readers follow. Whether you are writing from joy, hurt, or sadness, you'll find your triumphs, even the smallest, resound.

If you are using this book with a desire to write but no topic in mind, or with a desire to write about specific experiences in your life, the "write" questions and the writing exercises introduced for each essay style will help you find surprises. You will learn to write from experience even when you don't yet know exactly what in that experience is significant. Each time you explore one of the forms of essay writing, you will enter a "writing patch" inside yourself, a place where images and details arrive to help you grow the "experience plant" and see it bloom.

Realize That "Bad" Writing Is the Opportunity for Good Writing

When you write in the shadows of fear (and most of us have at least some of those shadows when it comes to writing), your writing may go on and on, like a boring teacher, never distinguishing the important details from the unimportant ones. Your writing may get so busy screaming, like an hysteric, about how you think you *ought* to feel that it can't evoke what you're really feeling. Or your writing may flit from one topic to another like a social butterfly without examining anything difficult.

Accept that sometimes the boring teacher, the hysteric, or the social butterfly will come into your writing. Your job is not to worry about their presence, but to learn to hear them covering or circumventing true experience. Using the three-step response method I introduce, you will learn to recognize the opportunity to cut away words that distort your true voice. You will honor whatever images and details are most important to your experience.

Say "I"

You may have had writing teachers who told you never to write "I" in an essay or to keep the number of times you wrote the word to a minimum. If you took that advice to heart, you may have stopped writing. As you stopped, you probably wondered from whom your writing might originate if not from an "I." If you kept on writing, you may have twisted and turned phrases so they appeared as if "I" never wrote them at all. After all those maneuvers to eradicate any evidence that you actually wrote your material, your meaning was probably quite blurred.

Just as you dream your own dreams, you live your own experiences. You are the filter for what you see, hear, taste, touch, and smell in this world. It is not only okay to report," I watched the leaves of the poplar trees blowing silver side up in the wind as my father told me my grandmother was dying," it is imperative for good writing. You must own your experience, every detail of it, to write well about it.

Each piece of experience builds into a bigger piece of experience. When you report where you are, what you see, taste, touch, feel and smell, you also release what is inside of you, the pattern of what you have learned. It is as if elements of the inside experience attach themselves to specific places on the outer landscape. That the leaves were silver side up as I heard the news of my grandmother's dying leads me as writer to other elements of my experience—the silver of my grandmother's hair and her temper blowing like strong wind. If you are sensitive to all experience, no matter how small, you are more deeply informed, and this information leads you to discovery.

When you are writing, do not worry about how often you use the word I. Use it as much as you need to. Just as you can weed out other words you no longer need when your work is nearing completion, so you can weed out extra "I's" by combining sentences or editing out phrases. It is very easy to take out what is no longer needed at the end. It is much harder to give yourself enough material to work with at the beginning. Say "I." This word lets you speak from your experience.

Recognize that Writing is a Formal Affair

The essay comes in eight styles: description; narration; how to; comparison and contrast; division and classification; definition; cause and effect and, finally, argument and persuasion.

An understanding of each style's structure (its strategies and components) will help you create writing that moves along gracefully—writing that helps you and the reader gain insight from your life events. In your life, things happen and you see and you do and you go. However, recounting what happened, what you saw, where you went, and what you did doesn't by itself aid you in discovering and communicating the *experience* you have gained from those happenings. It is the structure of the styles you are using in your work that becomes, both for you and your readers, a bridge to your learning, insights, and wisdoms.

In this book, essay styles introduced in later chapters make use of styles introduced in earlier ones. The patterns of thinking you engage to use each style are more elaborate as you move through them. However, it's not that you use one style over another to be more profound. The description essay style, which comes first in this book, creates essays that are just as profound as those created using the argument essay style, which comes last. Knowing all the styles gives you the *dexterity* with which to fully find and communicate the *range* of your human experience.

Here is an excerpt from the writing of a man in his mid-thirties who was assessing his life. Since he wrote without making good use of the styles available for the craft of essay writing, he thwarts his own search for self-discovery:

I am feeling terribly relaxed and thoughtful just now. The sea is rolling slowly toward the gray horizon just after sunset. I stare at it for hours. It is my Mantra. My life has not been a great joy of late. My job is taking more and more and giving me very little nourishment for the spirit. I wander back and forth across the Atlantic in a continuous twilight fog of jet lag with no direction. I can see that now in a moment of clarity.

I have been floating on a ship in the Gulf of Guinea off the Niger Delta for the last five days. Five quiet unhurried days waiting for equipment to be calibrated and parts to arrive. I can understand how a life at sea becomes so addictive to sailors. Such a soothing effect it has. No telephones, no traffic, no panic decisions. Just the rocking of a big cradle.

The seas are very calm today, almost glassy at times, but visibility is very poor. This is the time of year when northeast winds blow down from the Sahara carrying a very fine dust that fills the air. They call it the Harmatten. I like the name. It can last for days and becomes quite distracting, but it does cool down the otherwise steamy temperatures.

Each of the three paragraphs begins with information about being relaxed: he is relaxed and thoughtful; he is floating on a ship; the sea is calm. However, after the first sentence in each paragraph, the author gives information that contrasts with his stated mood. There is fog of jetlag, waiting for equipment, and the presence of dust and heat. The sea has lulled this writer for five days and now that he is writing about it, his first impulse is to gloss over his emotions by glossing over the dangers of being at sea (don't sailors make panic decisions and face difficult situations onboard?). This writer's easy life is taking place in fog and high temperatures. The writer can't get beyond being stuck in the calm of the sea even as his heart (and ours) is ready to motor into the rolling and difficult waves of life's trials.

If this writer understood the structure of description or narration, comparison and contrast, or some of the other essay styles I share in this book, he would be able to use his experience at sea to make a discovery about himself. The reader would experience not only the discovery, but the author's process of uncovering a hidden truth.

Silence Internal Voices That Keep You from Writing

Sometimes, imagined critics chant, "Your writing isn't good enough." Sometimes, the constant demands of life yell that your writing is not important enough to devote time to. Sometimes deep hurts that you haven't yet spoke about seem to say, "Don't mention it; let sleeping dogs lie."

All of these messages result from worrying that no one will be interested in what you have to say as an essayist. To help free yourself from this worry remember that even professionals succumb to it. Scholar and essayist Joseph Epstein claimed that each time he wrote his regular personal essay for *The American Scholar,* he wondered if the readers of the magazine would mutter to themselves about it being him again or, more terrifying, think, "Who cares!" Where, Epstein wondered, "does the personal essayist acquire the effrontery to believe—and, more astonishing still, to act on the belief—that his or her interests, concerns, quirks, passions matter to anyone else in the world?" If the "world is too rich, too various, too multifaceted and many-layered for a fellow incapable of an hour's sustained thought to hope to comprehend it," Epstein pondered, how could anyone care what he had to say? Despite his fear of the audience, he knew he wrote because he had "hope against hope" that he could "chip away at true knowledge by obtaining some modicum of self-knowledge."

Epstein warned, though, to "fight off adopting the notion of being in any way a star, at center stage," because the essay is most profound when it is modest. Be wary of thinking you are more interesting when you are didactic. An overly professorial tone will actually place you the writer center stage through an insistence on being right. The essay has come a long way from its beginnings in American literature, when clergymen used it to spread the influence of the pulpit from moral issues to intellectual and literary concerns. Today, being over-insistent and humorless about knowing what is right and demanding that readers see it your way is out of fashion. "Here," today's essays say, "Come and see that all of us are really very human and though flawed most loveable when we seek a way to connect and appreciate."

If you are afraid of speaking your truths and hurts, remember that the existential moment of the essay demands that we see beyond where we are at the moment. The essayist uses writing to better understand essence and move into new territory. Sometimes the old hurts don't want to allow the essayist to write through them to someplace new.

Writing essays means to consider life and in that consideration, to set down the glow of one or more of life's sparks. Whether you are writing about making and losing friends, moving, hearing children's nightmares and stories, remembering parents and grandparents, planting gardens, exploring new places, walking to the same old store, or about war, abuse, and sad neglect, you are writing not only to capture life's meaning but to capture the very struggle you endure to stay in touch with it. Because we all need to be reminded of how to do this, every essay you write, no matter the topic, has value to a wide range of readers as well as to you.

Get Response

Many writers find it helpful to join a writer's group. Having an audience that meets regularly and is committed to writing affirms writers in their work. Everyone in your group does not actually have to be a writer. Anyone truly interested in experience and in responding to writing can be helpful. Although even one person is valuable for getting response to your work, two or more are better since you will get a variety of responses to consider.

Whether you are reading your work to one friend, forming a new writer's group, or working with an existing one, familiarize those you trust to hear your drafts with the method of responding I present in Chapter III. I developed the three-step response method after years of finding out what goes wrong for new writers as they put words together on a page and finding out what goes wrong for writers when others evaluate their work or offer "constructive" criticism. Responding to writing is different from telling someone how to fix writing. No one who wants to write should flounder and fall away because of criticism and old schoolroom jargon.

When you share your writing, whether with a single friend or in a group, be sure to share only the words on the page. Listen to the response without defending or explaining your work. Don't verbally fill in points. If you explain, the responses will be to what you have said, not to what you wrote. Your job is to develop your writing, not your explaining.

If you do not have anyone nearby with whom you want to share your writing, there are other ways to get response. You can find writers discussion groups online, and you can use email and snail mail with people you know or meet at conferences, regional workshops or at your local library's or bookstore's writing circles. Check sites like writers.com, absolutewrite.com, writersdigest.com and writingitreal.com for information and links to groups online. A written form of the three-step response method works very well.

There are also methods for working without outside response or before you seek it. Writers often read their work into tape recorders. After a break of at least an hour, they play the piece back to themselves and take notes to give themselves response. Writers might record the response as well and listen to themselves before they revise. Other ways of creating some distance from your work in order to become a better responder to work-in-progress include retyping it to get a new feel for it and using a puppet while reading the work aloud so the work seems to be coming from someone else's mouth and mind. Some people mail their manuscript to themselves so that by the time it arrives back in their hands it seems like something they have not seen before.

Whether you use a group, one trusted listener, pals on the Internet, tape recorders, puppets, or the U.S. mail, what matters is that you detach yourself from your own words long enough to hear them as someone else might. You want an opportunity to learn what is memorable to readers, what they feel, and what they are curious to know more about. Then you will be in a good position to begin revisions.

Writing essays is a lot like hiking through a wilderness. Just as a compass helps indicate the direction to travel and careful observation helps you figure out a way there, your inner voice aided by the response of your listeners indicates the path of your essay.

An essay helps you learn—in a more complete way—what it is you have actually experienced. Unlike journal writing done for your eyes only, essay writing forces you to shape your experience so it can be fully understood by others. Only when another can receive the full insight, wisdom, and learning of your experiences can you truly see and feel that insight, wisdom, and learning yourself. This is the moment of the two-way mirror.

After you read the sample essays and discussions, take time in each chapter to do the exercises. This will help you prime the pump for writing in each style. After writing your first drafts, seek response, and then use the response to help as you develop your essays.

Chapter III

The Description Essay

Write Question #1: For what person, place, event, or object do I have strong feelings of love or of hate?

The boundaries of our world shift under our feet and we tremble while waiting to see whether any new form will take the place of the lost boundary or whether we can create out of this chaos some new order.
—Rollo May
The Courage to Create

Good essay writing requires good descriptions. How can readers hold on to what an author says in any piece of writing if they can not see what the author sees, hear what she hears, taste what she tastes, smells what she smells, and touch what she touches? When you sit down to write, you may become afraid that you are not up to describing a person, place, event or object so a reader can experience what you experienced. You may think that your own experience is vague and disappointing when you write it as compared to when you remember it.

Learning the elements of a good description essay and practice conjuring details and images that appeal to the senses will help you overcome these feelings and be able to offer your readers (as well as yourself) the written experience of the people, places, events and objects in your life. Although you can certainly use the description form even if you don't have particularly strong feelings, when it comes to the personal essay, it is the strength of your feelings as a motivating force for your description and desire to share experience that reaches readers. Sometimes, as you write, you discover that you have way more complex feelings and experience associated with a person, place, event or object than you thought.

In addition to gaining insight through writing the description style personal essay, once you learn the elements of good description, you will be better able to include description as a basic ingredient of the seven other essay styles.

To begin, ask, "For what person, place, event, or object in my life do I have strong feelings of love or of hate?" If you already have an area of life you know you want to write about because of strong feelings, it is time to organize those feelings around specifics and create a new order out of the chaos of unarticulated feelings. For instance, divorce, parenting, illness, fighting in a war, or visiting a foreign country may be among your topics of personal interest. Ask yourself: "What do I hate or love about my divorce, my parenting, my illness, my war experiences, or my visit to a foreign country?" Don't allow yourself to answer with generalities such as, "I love or hate the freedom of being divorced, the parental feeling of being in charge of someone, the limiting feeling illness creates, or the scared feeling of taking orders from an inept sergeant." Answer with something specific. You love or hate the way your ex-spouse looked when you argued, the way your baby smiled when you tickled him in parent-infant classes, the way your neighbors have come through for you, the way a superior gave orders in the army, the way mossy rocks felt in a stream bed in France.

"I hate the slippery mossy rocks and the way they will not allow me a foothold," might be your answer to "What do I hate about my trip to France?" Or if you love your trip to France, you might find yourself saying, "I love the bread everywhere—under the arm of the man returning home by bicycle, on the blue and white checkered tablecloth with no plate beneath it, in the windows of the boulangeries."

If you have no particular topic in mind, simply ask, "What do I love or hate?" You might be surprised to suddenly remember the county fair you went to each year as a child, the old Ford pickup still parked in your driveway, your grandmother's jam, your grandfather's woodshop, your first piano teacher, or dune buggies in an Oregon state park.

Pick one of your subjects and list the smells, tastes, sounds, sights and textures of the event, place, or person you have chosen to describe. In your writing, you will have to smell, taste, hear, see and touch what you are writing about *as if for the first time*. This requires that you avoid *telling* your attitude about your topic and instead let the images and details of the experience speak for themselves.

I remember a little boy who attended one of my Saturday morning writing classes. He wrote, "My teacher is gross." I told him I understood how he felt about his teacher, but I did not get the *picture* of a gross teacher. He then wrote, "When she is angry, my teacher looks like a horse with the reins pulled back." Now there was something for me to see! And there was something for him to see as well. His teacher scared him.

Once your senses "get" the tastes, sounds, smells, feel, and look of things, you and your readers will experience the subtle and complex feelings that inspired your interest in your subject.

Before you begin writing your description essay, look closely at the two sample essays I've included in this chapter and do the exercises I provide to gather the sensory images and details you will need for writing your essay.

When you think about a person, place, event, or object you care about, the strong feelings you have may make it hard to figure out what to include and what to leave out. How can you make the person, place, event, or object real to the reader? How can you relay what your subject really means to you? When you are "in touch" with your topic through the senses, the images of your description essay allow the meaning, the feelings, to come through. As you read the sample essays in this chapter, notice how the emotion builds from the particulars included by the essayists.

In addition, notice that part of what keeps you as reader involved in the subject of a description essay is the spatial organization. Authors of description essays allow readers to understand where they are physically by organizing sensory details according to location.

Example Description Essays

In his essay, "The Locker Room," Roy Nims describes a place he hated because of the great discomfort he experienced there. As you read, note what you see, hear, taste, touch, feel and smell on your trip with Nims. You might even make columns on a page for each of the senses and list the images from the essay that employ each sense in the appropriate column. Where is Nims when he gives the reader each of the images? Where he is as the essay continues creates the spatial order. When you are finished reading, think about what happens for you as the essay's "passenger." Ask, "Why does Nims revisit this place in his essay and how might that help him?"

The Locker Room

I'd entered the locker room through the door marked BOYS ONLY. It was across the narrow hallway from the gymnasium on the east side of the ground floor. Once inside, I'd be surrounded by a constantly present cloud of thick steam; the shower room to the back kept the air hot and humid. Whenever I had a cold, which was often, I found this steam particularly annoying. My already swollen and squinted eyes would swell and squint further. I'd breathe only in short, shallow breaths in order to prevent disruption of whatever quiet my clogged sinuses were managing. Such congestion would make me vertigo stricken whenever I leaned down to the small square compartment, which could barely contain my clothing.

My locker was to the far back of the room and to the left. To reach it, I'd walk past five or six aisles of tall rows of small square lockers. These aisles were always filled with long-haired, half-naked boys constantly sneering and guffawing. Very few seconds passed that there wasn't a shoe, towel or some such item of personal property aloft in the steamy air. The slamming of lockers echoed continuously off of the cement walls, which hadn't been painted in so long their color was indiscernible. It seemed such chaos that I couldn't help but assume the defensive attitude of a trapped mammal anticipating, at any time, an attack from an undetermined direction.

The boys at that age exhibited little in the way of compassion. The zoo of the locker room served as their arena for whatever cruelties they found entertaining. They were fond of carrying switch-blades, if for no other purpose, to snap open in front of the faces of those smaller than themselves and see the blade reflected in their eyes.

As ages ranged from about twelve to fifteen, there was quite a span of levels of physical development represented. Thus, those boys not yet honored by puberty received vicious and repeated ridicule.

I recall being one of the unfortunates. My mother had been neurotically puritanical in shaping our family's attitudes toward nudity, and for me to strut about the shower room naked as a jaybird was never a matter of joy. It was certainly less than helpful that the embarrassment be infinitely augmented by the crude jeers from older boys concerning my genital development or seeming lack thereof. I would pretend to ignore it and concentrate on the sound of my wet feet slapping the cold cement floor as I made my way to my locker.

I would usually dress facing the dark corner, as discreetly as possible. On one such occasion, I was targeted for a particular amount of abuse. While still naked, I was too slow to stop a fellow from grabbing my athletic supporter, running off and tossing it out the door into the populated hallway.

Everyone in the locker room roared with laughter as I pulled on my ragged bell bottomed jeans. Dressing as rapidly as possible, I dropped my cotton shirt into a puddle of water on the floor.

When finally dressed, I walked as inconspicuously as possible into the brightly lit hallway. The student body had been transformed to one hundred percent female. A number of boys had raced to the locker room doorway to point and screech and clarify to all confused observers the precise nature of the situation. There was my jockstrap in the middle of the floor. I walked over to it. Hardly breathing, I picked it up, my wet shirt clammily staying to my right side and armpit. I felt feverish. My face was flushed and red hot. My heart was beating inconsistently. The boys at the door were nearly in tears and a few girls were giggling as I crowded my way back into the locker room. When inside, I found that my things had been thrown all about the room, on top of the rows of lockers and in trash cans. My jacket had been thrown in the shower and drenched.

Everyday someone was the victim. If the victimization wasn't physical with bodies or property abused in some fashion, it was verbal and grotesque. There must have been a hundred names for a faggot.

There wasn't a time I was there that my attention wasn't fully bent on getting out as quickly as possible. I welcomed the feeling of finally lacing my shoes snugly around my cold feet, which were probably still wet, as I'd toweled myself hurriedly. This final step of dressing done, I'd get up from the bench and waste no time in reaching the door, usually carting too many things and never stopping to look to the side.

I'd welcome the relative freedom of motion offered by the hall-ways. The lighting was noticeably better and made me feel as if I'd emerged from an abysmal den of mental illness. It was so unex-plainable as to make me feel, in a matter of seconds, that I couldn't possibly be remembering it correctly.

How the Writer Makes a Discovery and Shares It in "The Locker Room"

We enter the locker room just as Nims did—through the door marked BOYS ONLY. Once inside the door (located precisely, we are told, on the east side of the ground floor), we experience the in-terior of the locker room through our nerve endings when the speaker tells us how the humid air affected him.

In the second paragraph, more of our senses are involved. Now we not only see and feel the interior of the locker room, we hear it as well—locker doors slamming against cement walls.

And once we focus on the boys in there, we are well into the emotional tone of this essay. Our speaker is among the threatened and is acutely aware of his wet feet slapping the cold cement floor. Say that last phrase aloud. The phrase's rhythm and sound emulate the unrelenting pain of walking in that room before those boys! The writer, in owning and remembering his experience precisely, naturally achieves the sound that conveys emotional meaning. (This happens when you are writing well.)

The painful and helpless vulnerability continues, growing in in-tensity for two short paragraphs and one long one, until even the speaker's jacket, an article of clothing representative of the world outside the gym and its locker room, is effected.

Having toured the locker room with the author, we learn about the others and the insults they endured. Then, like in a film, we get a shot of the speaker finishing the last detail of dressing—tying his shoes on feet left wet from rushing. We can assume that he rushed everyday he was required to use that locker room.

Next we go out into the hallway where the lighting is better and where our speaker can no longer believe that the actions, the fear, and the hurt inside the locker room were real. Such putting away of the horror of that room was probably the only way he could endure. The lit hallway seems worlds away from the steamy, dangerous locker room. We feel both the truth of the horror and the truth of the need to downplay that horror in order to go on in an environment that demanded the same bad experience day after day. Writing about the horror, Roy no longer has to downplay it; he seeks it out and evokes it with every detail he includes. I believe that pushing the locker room events to the surface of his memory helped Nims work himself free of lingering embarrassment.

In her essay, "Dreams of Going," Barbara Stahura utilizes the description form to describe a place she remembers fondly. As you read, think about the author's way of situating us in her room during her childhood. What are the details she shares? Look at her use of lists to let us into her world as well as her technique of zeroing in on two sounds, "First came . . ." and "Then there was my other sound" to offer rich description of her emotional state in childhood. When you have finished the essay, ask why Stahura wrote it—of course the reason is deeper than to describe a place she knows and loves, but she doesn't discover that reason until the writing is on the page.

Dreams of Going

On cool summer mornings, curled under a cotton sheet and a pink chenille bedspread, I often awoke gradually, rather than to Mom's quiet call of, "It's time to get up, sleepyhead." Before my eyes opened, my mind would slowly come alert, wordlessly aware that the confusion of the day had not yet begun. As I rested in the gentle darkness of closed eyelids, my ears would accept the familiar sounds flowing through the screened window next to me. Two in particular spin threads of comfort even now, decades later. They inspired a longing I could not then articulate, although I believe I have now deciphered their code.

I'm not sure why, among all the waking-up sounds, I searched for just these two, as if I were listening to a symphony and awaiting only the most delicate thrum of the violins. My two "best sounds," typically scorned as so much noise, were the hum of the nearby highway and the whistles of the many trains that rumbled through Hammond.

At this hour of the day, all the sounds I heard through the open window were muted. Perhaps it was my delicious sense of coziness that softened them; more likely, it was the cool, damp air of those early summer mornings. I would hear the rustle of the tall lilac bushes that bloomed sweetly and extravagantly on the boundary between our backyard and the Millers'. I would hear the breeze-brush of the leaves on the four maple trees Daddy had planted, one in each corner of the yard, and the gentle cacophony of songbirds mingled with the harsh barking of neighborhood dogs. Sometimes black and yellow bees buzzed as they bumbled against the screen. But my ears passed over these sounds of nature. As a very shy, timid girl frequently confused by living in a world I often could not understand, I was greedy for the two sounds that somehow came to both anchor me and inspire deliverance.

The first came from the highway. A steady, gentle hum rose from the thousands of vehicles that traveled it each day. The two miles between this main artery into Chicago and our house on Maplewood Avenue blanketed honking horns, screeching tires, and the gear rumbles of behemoth trucks. The early morning breeze carried only the peaceful drone of movement and travel, of life on its daily course. The people whose vehicles orchestrated this sound were going to work, to school, to visit friends. Somehow I sensed they were never confused—how could they navigate this busy highway if they were? They were confident of their purpose.

They knew which direction to take, how to be in the world. At the time, I didn't know I could be other than how I was, but I nevertheless wanted to be like them.

This traffic hum was faint, yet there it was, every day, even weekends, and I came to count on its presence. Early morning was the only time I ever heard it. Once I got out of bed or said even a word, the spell was broken: It never appeared again all day. So I held still, hardly breathing, ears alert.

Then there was my other sound.

In those days, dozens of trains passed through Hammond on their way to steel mills, factories, and Chicago. Sometimes literally a mile long, these trains hauled everything from milk to Fords. They would block traffic all over town, at any time of day, stopping and reversing, then slowly moving forward again, while anxious drivers honked their horns and muttered or cursed.

But on those cool, lazy mornings, before the pollution haze settled on the sky and abrupt daytime noises took over, I never thought of those rude trains. All I knew were their whistles far away, muted by the dewy air. Like the highway sounds, these disembodied wails also represented life's movement, in which I, still a little girl, could not yet actively participate. But their distant sighs inspired the fantasy that I, too, could travel to another city and become someone new: a confident girl who was neither painfully shy nor too smart, who was not the ugly duckling belonging nowhere, nor the one who tried too hard to be good, and who read about life instead of living it, because inside a book she was safe.

Now I am a grown woman, much more confident and outgoing, with only a lingering shyness. I have traveled highways and ridden trains, in truth and in imagination, to become the person I am. I am still smart, and glad of it. I still try to be good, but not so hard and not because parents and nuns tell me I have to. I still feel safe within the pages of a book and am even trying to write my own. Sometimes I wake early in my grown-up bed, windows open around it, and hear the distant vehicular hum and slow train whistles of my new city. It is then I remember that little girl under the window, safe in her bed and still fuzzy with sleep, listening to sounds and dreaming of going.

How the Writer Makes a Discovery and Shares It in "Dreams of Going"

How does Barbara Stahura travel in this description essay? By leaping from one auditory image to another. First, there is the call of the speaker's mother, than the ambient sounds outside the window, and finally with a little work, the sounds the speaker wants to hear above the others, the vehicles and trains. Stahura offers a full description of one sound and then of the other. The descriptions draw us in because Barbara makes effective use of the senses. "My two 'best sounds,'" the author calls them, as a child would name the way she possesses her world. "Then there was my other sound," she writes after filling us in on the first one. "Now I am a grown woman," begins her last paragraph. The elegant transitions keep this essay focused and lulling.

As she introduces them, she explains what she had emotionally attached to each sound and how each symbolized her deepest life wishes. When she is done describing her youthful waking to those sounds and evaluates her life, she sees that she has fulfilled the call of the sound and seems to take renewed courage from hearing such sounds outside her "grown-up" window. The moment of self-evaluation through memory works to guarantee that the writer understands how she fulfilled her dreams of going and yet remained herself.

Locating Your Own Description Material

Start by asking the "write" question for beginning a description essay: For what person, place, object or activity do I have strong feelings of love or hate? Search for material using the exercises that follow.

Clustering

Clustering, as introduced by Gabriel Rico in *Writing the Natural Way*, is a method that can help you come up with some unexpected answers to your question. Begin with one of the following words—"people," "places," "things," or "events"—circled in the center of a blank piece of paper. If, for example, you choose to start with the word "people" in the center, draw lines from that word to the names of particular people you know and have known and about whom you have strong feelings and draw a line from each name to the center word. Then circle it. Next draw lines from the name to particular images you associate with that person. Circle each image. Pretty soon you will have a bunch of balloons on your page.

When you feel interest in a particular grouping of the cluster, begin a new cluster and associate images and memories for this new subject. For instance, clustering about places I loved, I remembered my back fence in early spring when the tulips along it are in bloom. Then clustering around the phrase "vanilla tulips along the back fence," I gathered more and more images from the recesses of my memory.

A word about the circling—it is the major difference between Rico's clustering activity and other prewriting activities you may have come across, like mind mapping, brainstorming, and branching. The act of circling the associations you make, according to Rico, frees your mind from its usual habits and opens you up as a writer to deeper, more unexpected material. I have experienced this as an extremely productive way to find and to center myself in my chosen material. Circling is a simple act, but it is a physical way of keeping the mind from getting too logical and blocking out useful associations. More than that:

> Everything
> the Power of the World does
> is done in a circle.
> —Black Elk, Oglala Sioux,
> *Catch the Whisper of the Wind*

You may have a hard time thinking in circles instead of in lines. Most of us were taught to brainstorm by listing, and that can be useful. But when you are gathering, nothing should seem more or less important than anything else that occurs to you. Lists tend to make things look prioritized or organized. The inventive part of your brain doesn't want to be hemmed in this early. Think of circle making as a way to create a net into which your images will swim. The order in which these images come into the net doesn't matter. The more you practice this approach, the more images you'll catch. If it feels uncomfortable, keep practicing. You will be delighted with what swims in when you least expect it.

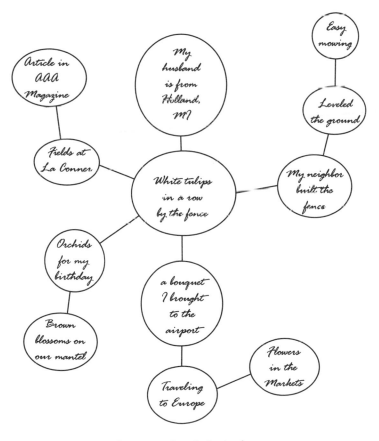

An example of clustering

Freewriting

After you do the first clustering exercise, a particular person, place, event, or object from the circles should most draw your attention. Do a second cluster as I did to recover more details and images about your subject. When you feel you have gathered enough to write for ten minutes, do so without worrying about what you are saying or what you will do with what you are saying. You might keep your cluster nearby to remind you of some details but once you start your freewrite many more will come. Note: if one particular person, place, event, or object doesn't seem more interesting than the others, chose one just for the sake of doing the exercise. Once you've done the exercise, your writing mind will gain confidence in the results of clustering and freewriting.

When you do your freewrite, write in complete sentences, without erasing or crossing out. Keep your pen moving; keep your fingers on the keyboard. If you can't think what to say next, just repeat what you already said. The idea here is to keep writing. Your mind and memory will eventually jump to a new image. Writing with momentum keeps your writing mind active and engaged rather than inert, overwhelmed, and silent. The purpose of the freewrite is to loosen you up, to get some writing out of your fingers, and to prove to you that your writing can take on a life of its own. (Peter Elbow has a full discussion of this process in his books, *Writing Without Teachers* and *Writing With Power*.)

Clustering and freewriting create room for the past and the present to intertwine. Freewrites are a place to immerse yourself in memories without worrying about how they will go together in a finished piece of writing. Without worrying, you will be able to access more and more of your material.

Here's the freewrite I did from my cluster. You will see that the trunk of images about my neighbor building the fence with an edge in mind and my disrupting that clean edge becomes the main thought. I use some of the other information, like traveling to

Europe, only to help tell why I don't know what color the tulips will be. When you freewrite from a cluster, you do not have to use everything you conjured and you can add more images as they come up.

Sheila's Freewrite

Vanilla tulips stand straight against the cedar back fence. Not all of the tulip buds are open, though, and I wonder if the unopened ones might be pink or yellow. And why are they going to bloom later than the white ones? A year and a half ago, I put all the bulbs in and at blooming time, I left to visit my daughter in Europe. When I came home, the tulips were finished. I don't remember now which kinds of tulips I chose or in what pattern I planted them.

So often I change the course I've made or someone else has made for me. My neighbor built the fence and leveled the ground right up to, making an edge for easy lawn mowing. Then I put the bulbs in and now at least in spring, we have to hand trim the grass around the tulips, under the boughs of the cherry trees which blossom then drop their petals like opals over the ground.

When the tulips finish this year, I'll braid their leaves, which will make it easier for whomever mows the lawn. But underground, the bulbs will be gathering nutrition for next spring's burst of color, forcing us again away from easy mowing.

If you have trouble moving from the cluster to the freewrite, leave the cluster in front of you as you freewrite. Take a second to glance at it if you feel yourself slowing the pen or fingers down. Grab whatever image your eye falls on and write it into what you are saying. Don't worry if you contradict yourself or change topics mid-stream. This is a momentum-building exercise and a way for you to learn to trust that the act of writing creates order from chaos by attaching certain images to other images. If freewriting is hard for you, practice just moving the pen with no commitment whatsoever to the sense the freewrite may or may not make. Part of writing is keeping writing.

This Is An Essay

Now that you have allowed your writing self to write, it is time to think about coaching your writing self to use images that come in through the senses. I have created an exercise to help you gather sensory images about your subject. It comes from a poem by the late Washington State poet Charles Proctor, who described a near-fatal collision by starting every line of a poem with, "This is a poem about." In this way, he could finish each line with a specific image of the moments leading up to and through the event. Taking things on moment-by-moment lends itself to gathering and collecting images without fear of what you might "do with them."

The form of the poem—the listing and repetition of the phrase, "This is a poem"—offered Charles a structure. He didn't have to worry about where to start each new sentence. Using the topic in your freewrite, make a list like this using the phrase, "This is an essay about" to begin each line. You will find the rhythm of the repetition is like casting seeds, and that at the end of each line, images and details germinate like seedlings.

Sometimes, it takes practice to get past tacking general words onto the end of the sentences. Concentrate on using the sensory details essential for vivid writing. Focus on the details that connect you to your subject through your five senses. If you had been Roy Nims writing about the locker room, you might have listed: This is an essay about air thick with steam. This is an essay about socks and underwear aloft in that air. This is an essay about my jock strap thrown from the room to the hallway. You would not have written, "This is an essay about feeling overwhelmed." Make the details and images create feelings without naming them. If you were Barbara Stahura, you might have written: This is an essay about listening to car horns and train whistles from my bed in our home on Maple

Avenue. This is an essay about the sound of bees outside my window. This is an essay about pollution haze and day noises.

Go ahead. Write a "This is an essay about" on your topic. Try to make it at least a page long. If you are writing or typing and don't feel like writing the beginning to the sentences over and over, at least say them to yourself out loud. Physically experiencing this repetition, whether in your fingers or on your tongue, will help call forth the images you need to immerse yourself in the remembered experience.

Comparative Thinking

Another powerful exercise is to describe one thing as if it were something else quite unrelated. Bringing the two together refreshes your experience of your subject. This kind of thinking helps you describe people, places and events with details that capture the five senses.

Remember how it hit you when you read that the little boy's teacher looked like a horse with the reins pulled back? When you use "like" to make a comparison, you create a simile; when you exclude the "like" and say one thing *is* another thing, you make a metaphor. Both strategies offer opportunities to put yourself and your readers at the heart of your experience.

Describing Birkenstock sandals I wrote, "The straps over my feet are two highway overpasses." The meat in oxtail soup looks like already chewed Wrigley's spearmint gum to a character in Christi Killien's *All of the Above.* "When I'm in the bathtub, I'm like the seed inside an avocado," a woman said in a writing workshop.

Making comparisons becomes easier if you practice. Propose beginnings at one time of day: a window is like . . ., children in a classroom are like . . ., a doorknob is like . . .. And at another time of day, write endings: a window is like a movie screen; children in a classroom are like a flower garden; a doorknob is like a knee. You can also do this exercise as a game with friends, students, family or pen pals, verbally, over email, or by posting beginnings (on bulletin boards or refrigerators) for others to fill in.

This exercise keeps your mind flexible. If you continue to do it when you start writing your essay, you will see how similes and metaphors pop into your mind just when you need them to help you fully describe (show through the senses) your subject.

More about Detail and Images

Writing description *requires* that you use images from the five senses. Taste, smell, feel, sound, and appearance ultimately tell the story and do the work of describing. To say, "I was always stiff at Grandmother Sarah's house" does not describe rigidity. The following words *show* your stiffness:

> I always sat in the red overstuffed mohair sofa, my feet never reaching the floor, watching the white lace of my fancy Sunday anklets above the shiny patent leather of my Mary Janes. The pudgy fingers of my left hand crumpled and uncrumpled the lace that covered the sofa arm I sat up against, and I always noticed the dirt under my finger nails, black as my shoes, against the white of Grandmother's lace. I was like a snake without a safe place to molt an ill-fitting skin.

Try out sensory details that *show* what you are describing rather than words that merely *tell* your attitude. Details that are unique to the situation are the basic units of your writing. They are the substance that allows you to gather momentum, to go on, to build a route through your material, to find closure and discovery. Include them in overabundance in exercises when you are seeking your material. What did you taste, touch, feel, see, and smell in the situation you are describing? Where can a metaphor bring surprise and exactness to your description? If you feel like you are in a detail drought, stop and do a cluster about the particular image.

Writing Your Essay

If you haven't done a cluster yet to help you answer the "write" question for description, do it now. Continue with a freewrite for ten minutes on the person, place, object, or activity that interests you this time. Do the "This is an Essay About" exercise, if you haven't yet. Practice using metaphors to describe your subject. Remember the power of detail and images and use them abundantly.

After you have done this preliminary invention work, go back and examine how the example essays begin and how the authors organized them: face-to-face with the entrance to a dreaded place in one, and, in the other, lying in bed in a place the speaker longs to leave.

One opening idea might come from the famous essayist E.B. White, who began a description essay called "Twins," about the first few moments of two fawns' lives, with a statement of how he came to be there:

On a warm, miserable morning last week we went up to the Bronx Zoo to see the moose calf and to break in a new pair of black shoes. We encountered better luck than we had bargained for.

With all your exercise work in front of you, find any way you think might work to begin. Start with what you see when you think about what you are describing. Or start with why you went there. Then continue drafting your description essay from your beginning to whatever ending you can find.

Developing the Draft

Put your draft aside for a while to get some distance from the sound of the writing that is fresh in your ears. Every writer needs to do this to return to work. When you have distance, you can better recognize what you have to revise from the sounds in your draft.

As in music, repetition, beat, rhythm, base lines, and pitch are important. They communicate feeling, lend enjoyment to readers, and establish trust between the readers and the writer. No matter how mundane and of this world the essay writer's thoughts are, sincerity, individuality, and honesty come through in the music the essay creates and that is what readers respond to. If the sounds are chiming, clanging, overly quieting or crashing about for little reason, as a writer, you can be sure that the essay has not found its stride. Learn to recognize cadences appropriate to your essay's mood, facilitate them, and let them bubble away in your work.

Most of us write personal essays because we believe we have something to say. While we search for words to say it, we often overlook something very important: we write because we want to hear ourselves say something. When we shift the emphasis from saying to hearing, we listen to our drafts and hear where we are out of tune. We can then return to our work with an emphasis on improving the sound of our words, and we will find we are better able to communicate what was difficult as we began our drafting.

Because hearing is important to developing final versions of essays, the lyric quality of words is as intriguing to the personal essayist as to the poet. Historically, the lyric genre of poetry meant one person singing of personal feelings. Until the Renaissance, lyric poems were accompanied by the music of a lyre; to this day the most impressive written works catch cadences that please, tease, and strike the ear. Learn to recognize when you are stifling sound in your work. Good writing is not good writing because it looks like good writing. It is good writing because it sounds good.

Years ago, a student of mine wrote an essay about defining her adulthood by accepting the ways in which her life was different from how she always believed it would be. In a first draft, she wrote:

My father used to rise at the same time every morning, kiss my mother on the cheek and make his way for the train station to board the high-speed line for the city. He always looked so important and sure of himself dressed in his dark suit with his raincoat draped over his arm and his briefcase in hand. At night when he returned . . .

Do you hear the sound of the steady walk memory is taking via the author's words? Do you hear the almost brisk, regular rhythm of this memory's walk, as if it is moving toward something it feels is important to reach? Do you hear the beat of memory's footsteps?

The paragraph in this draft of the essay continued:

> . . . he would again kiss my mother on the cheek. I always melted when they kissed with a warm hopefulness that I too someday would bestow such loving affection on someone else's cheek.

Does this sound out of tune to you? Does the walk seem to end without reaching what it was striding toward? Phrasing like, "He would kiss my mother on the cheek again" would have kept the tempo; " . . . that I too someday would bestow" actually sounds like our speaker's feet have gone from making a little stumble to tangling up beneath her.

Hearing the discordance, my student shortened the part about her father's return leaving only, "At night when he returned, he would again kiss my mother on the cheek," and she began a new paragraph with:

> Mother and Dad always worked as a team around the house, she taking care of the meals and daily upkeep and my father's projects varying depending on what household improvement Mother felt was needed . . .

With the revision, at the "would again," I hear memory slowing a little, halting as the parents again kiss, but not stumbling or almost tripping, as it seemed to when the "bestow" phrase followed. The slowing down I experience has the sound of awe combined with a hovering wistfulness, as if the speaker wished her days would close this way as well. What is important here is not what the speaker felt then so much as what she is remembering to report now. And the rhythm of the music keeps the essay focused on making meaning in this way.

Although sometimes taking words out restores music, fixing the music often requires putting specific images in. In another essay, one about a fondly remembered beach house, my student wrote about her room with its trundle bed:

> I always slept on the lower bed, close to the floor so that my girl-friends who were scared of the monsters that roamed in the dark would know they'd devour me first and be too full to go on to them. The sound of the distant waves splashing against the surf kept me company at night. I was never scared.

The "I was never scared," repeats the sound of "company at night" with a syllable count and stresses that are the same. The musical effect of this repetition is to dull or fog away something important (and much more musical). Just as we are drawn into the sound of the waves and surf as the sound of company, we are reminded about being scared. Why? Certainly the music has already had us dance away from that emotion. It doesn't feel like we should go back to it.

Upon revision, my student wrote:

> I always slept on the lower bed, close to the floor so that my girl-friends who were scared of the monsters that roamed in the dark would know they'd devour me first and be too full to go on to them. The sound of the distant waves splashing against the surf and the breeze rustling through my curtains kept me company at night. The days ran into night and nights kept fulfilling their promise of returning the day.

The addition of "rolling" images and of sounds that echo the rhythmic waves allows the essay to offer the actual experience of being lulled instead of frightened. The very sound of the language allows the memory from girlhood to enter our ears the way the rustling curtain, waves, and days once flowed together for the speaker. That is the lyric at work—the music that offers both the feel and emotion of what is remembered.

The personal essay, no matter how prosaic and daily, uses the lyric aspects of language to embrace emotion and experience. The best personal essays allow your memories of people and events to merge with your current feelings and deliver a message about now as well as then.

If you listen closely to the music you make on the page, you will learn to create the sounds of exactly what you have experienced. Keep this in mind when you return to the page after gathering response to what you have written.

Get Response Using the Three-Step Response

Whenever you are developing drafts and revisions, asking trusted readers to respond to your work in three separate stages helps ensure that you receive the kind of feedback that facilitates your writing. Remember to allow your responders to focus on your writing. Don't speak while the responders are talking, no matter how much you want to. Let them respond only to what is on the page. You can take notes on what words, thoughts and explanations leap to your tongue. You will find them helpful as you return to drafting. After all in a group have offered response in the three steps, you might want to ask more questions about particular responses or something that you felt wasn't addressed. You might also feel like thanking the group for being such thorough readers.

Step One: Velcro Words

After you read a draft, your listeners first repeat the words and phrases that stuck with them. They do not tell you why the words stuck or even say, "I liked . . .." They merely repeat your words back as closely as they remember them. It will feel wonderful to you. All of us write to be heard, and there is no better way to affirm that you've been heard than to hear your own words from someone else's mouth. Not telling why the words stuck keeps the focus on your writing.

Step Two: Feelings

To warm up for this step, listeners can list as many emotions as they can think of. The more emotions they list, the more versatile and articulate they will become in responding to writing: gentle, harsh, lost, discovered, nostalgic, sentimental, fearful, reconciled, panicked, bored, surprised, thankful, in mourning, grief-stricken, at odds, defeated, successful, glib, surrendered, frustrated, warm, joyful, happy, dislocated, well-grounded, clear, cloudy, disappointed and resistant are but a small number of names for feelings.

After they feel confident that they can name many feelings, listeners might hear your draft again and then name feelings elicited by the subject and tone of your writing, feelings that are in keeping with the subject and subtext they hear in the draft. Frequently their responses include opposites: sadness and joy, displeasure at loss and surprise at opening up to new gain, and innocence and learning, for example. This kind of contradiction enriches the writing as it holds the yin and yang of experience and satisfies the listeners.

If someone writes about being stuck with twin two-year-olds in a long line of cars at U.S.-Canadian customs by using the simile that he felt like Mt. St. Helens right before she erupted, workshop members might report registering feelings of bottled up anger or unbearable frustration.

After listeners report the feelings they believe are in keeping with the writing's intentions, they report whatever discomfort occurs inside them because of phrasing and details that veer from the writing's seeming subject and subtext. For instance, if the writer with the two-year-olds in his car included a detail like, "My stomach felt like a pond under a clear blue sky" when he was writing about feeling like Mt. St. Helens, readers might report that the clear blue sky evoked calmness that surprised them in the context of what they registered as frustration. The writer decides if the metaphor is accurate or not. Maybe in the drafting process, the writer had felt frustrated but when he was with the kids, he had enjoyed being away from adult responsibilities. The writer might take the writing in a new direction based on listerners' reports of emotional confusion.

Listener responses about the feelings engendered by your draft will help you figure out how your writing is making contact with others. If listeners or readers report contradictory responses, you may realize there are simple ways to clear up the inadvertent confusion by making very small changes in wording. Or, as in the Mt. St. Helen's example, you may realize that your feelings are quite different than you thought they were and begin an extensive rewrite.

Listener and reader responses help all writers keep from spinning their wheels and meandering from their real subjects. If listeners are confused, if they feel ripped off, if they feel batted around in different directions, the words are causing that confusion, that theft, that assault. If such emotional journeys do not serve the author's real subject, the author must change the words. It's a "self-correcting" exercise, like learning to cut with scissors; no one teaches children to cut on the lines—they keep at it and one day their eye-hand coordination develops to the point where they can do it. Something like this is true in the drafting process for writing. Receiving feeling-level response helps you design your writing along the true lines of its emotional story.

Step Three: Curiosity

Finally, listeners tell the writer want they want to know more about and where in the writing they want to know it. These specifics indicate where more writing is required. When others want to know more, writers get insight into their real subject and where and how they may have skirted it. They often realize that what they skipped because they thought it might bore a reader is exactly what the reader wants to know or that they inadvertently skipped something just because they know their subject so well.

Receiving response in these three steps (Velcro words, feelings, and curiosity) will open up possibilities for your revisions, leaving you not only empowered to continue developing a piece of writing but eager to do so. The three-step response method encourages writing that is authentic, lively, and very much worth getting right.

About Resistance

Monitoring feelings can be a tiring business. Your listeners may not be used to paying close attention to what they are feeling as you read, let alone what they might name these feelings. Practice and patience will help your listeners gain dexterity in responding.

When responding to writing, precision—being "picky"—is a virtue. As a writer, you really don't want anything to get in the way of your reader's enjoyment and you want to hear what does. But listening to ways your drafts may not be working can prove difficult. What will help you listen well to the responses? First, you'll enjoy hearing what makes strong contact with others. Second, you'll be listening to feelings, not judgments. "I felt confused" is much gentler than "This sounds awkward" or "The writing is disorganized."

When a reader labels or judges your writing ("You are being repetitive," "This is wordy" and so on), you may feel anger and think, "How do they know anyway?" This reaction can block you from wanting to rework your writing. The three-step response is meant to help listeners give response in a way that circumvents this natural defend-against-labels attitude and promotes your readiness and enthusiasm for revision. Listening to the results of the three-step response, you will learn how your words line up with the content of what you are saying. However, if someone should send "you-messages" instead of "I-messages" in their response, convert the messages into something usable: "I feel overwhelmed by the number of words it took to let me know where the speaker is." "I found myself wanting to believe the writer but uncertain about why I should feel that way." "I kept getting lost and didn't know where I was." Hearing "I–statements" opens up possibilities for the writer in revision. Elicit them from your early readers (as well as from yourself) when you are revising and in need of direction.

When you work along these lines, you make it possible for your future audience to follow your thinking and feelings. As Lu Chi, an ancient Chinese poet, said:

> Emotion and reason are not two things:
> every shift in feeling must be read.
> —*The Art of Writing*
> translated by Sam Hamill

On Being Wary

One barrier to using the three-step response method is your own wariness about sharing your writing. You may be sensitive to what people think, afraid others will steal an idea and concerned that exposure will diminish your energy to write.

It is never wholly comfortable listening to people talk about your writing while you sit there, not saying a word. It is like having people talk in front of you about the clothes you are wearing. Be aware of your sensitivities, but don't let them interfere. The people who give responses are offering you a gift. Accept the gift. Later you can decide what you are going to do with it.

To work effectively with other writers, understand that cross-fertilization is a good thing. Writers are thieves in that they may end up writing about the same subjects as authors whom they admire. You must believe simultaneously that there are many, many ideas *and* that there is actually nothing new under the sun, only well wrought tales of the same old same-olds. Understand that your experience, even if similar to someone else's, will be different because it is told in your voice, from your life, as only you can write it.

Using the three steps, you will gain insight into where to "go from here" with your work. As one of my students said, "In college and high school, teachers always told me what was wrong with my work, but not where better work would come from." When you hear how a reader feels about your work—what sticks with them, what vaults them out of the experience you are describing, what bores them, what engages their curiosity— you will find yourself propelled to continue. Using the three-step response helps you move past negative internal chatter like, "I'm such a boring writer," "I don't know enough words to write well," or "Who do I think I am writing this?"

Henriette Klauser, author of *Writing on Both Sides of the Brain,* gives a wonderful example of the difference between nurturing self-talk and paralyzing self-criticism. When her son began to talk, everyone who heard him exclaimed about his "good talking." No one said he pronounced words wrong or used the wrong forms of pronouns and verbs. Who would criticize a child new to speech? But how we say similar things to ourselves when we are starting a new piece of writing! Can you imagine being so hungry you can hardly wait to eat dinner and at the same time talking to yourself about how you hold the fork wrong? Use the three steps of Velcro words, feelings, and curiosity to rethink how you speak to yourself about your writing. There are no wrong ways, only words that stick, feelings that get evoked and places to write more.

An important note: When something you feel committed to in your writing gets a negative response, examine it to discover why you have included it. Ask yourself what feeling it evokes for you. Sometimes messages from the unconscious are delivered to the wrong address. The message is fine, but it needs to be re-delivered to another location in the essay or even to another essay.

For an extended example of the three-step response method, see Appendix I (page 209), which is a recreation of the three-step dialogue between a student struggling with writing an essay and me. It illustrates in considerably more detail the intimate details of the three-step process.

Nurture Your Writing and Keep Drafting

In writing description always remind yourself to:

- Stay with the senses.
- Make comparisons that continue to share the experience as it was in the very moment you had it.
- Stay in those moments that interest you.
- Present experience itself. Your images have authority. They say, "This is how it was for me."
- Listen for the places where you may be keeping yourself from direct experience.

Doing these five things, you will discover why you were compelled to relive being with a particular person, holding or looking at a particular object or coming to a particular place or event. Write through as many drafts as it takes until you are satisfied that the subject is fully experienced by your readers.

Whenever you can, read each draft of your work aloud to others. No one needs to love the whole draft to be able to offer a valuable response using the three-step method. And no one needs to be an expert on writing! If you need some immediate response and don't have a writing group available, a neighbor or even a child can provide reactions with much to teach you.

Chapter IV

The Narration Essay

Write Question # 2: When have I lost (or found) someone, something or some opportunity?

> *The myth of the Fall portrays us all as exiles from the full human*
> *potential . . . History is the story of our efforts . . . to recover a unity we*
> *have intuited only in the fragments.*
>
> — Sam Keen
> *The Passionate Life: Stages of Loving*

Often things happen to you that seem like a story out of a book or out of a film and you want to write the story down in a way that will amuse or affect other people emotionally. Telling a story is called narration. Narration-style essays require the arrangement of experiences in an order that allows readers to understand how a situation began, developed, and was resolved. This order is often chronological, and the writer organizes events through time to come to new insight.

When you sit down to write narrations, you probably only know that you want to tell about the "time when . . ." You might not know the deeper reasons you want to write these stories, which usually have to do with finding or losing someone, something, or some opportunity. As you write the story, your writing leads you to new understanding about what specific losses and gains have meant to you.

The narration style uses the organization of events through time to make an emotional point. Like every essay style, it encompasses the sensory detail of good description, which creates a picture. Using chronology and description allows you to build essays that explore meaningful times and encounters and what you learned from them.

When writing personal stories, it sometimes seems that emotion skips town, leaving only events on the page that don't do justice to experience. You can overcome this lack of emotion by doing exercises from the description chapter before you write a narration essay as well as by using a new exercise I introduce later in this chapter.

How do you know where to start and where to stop your story? Writing a good story requires more than stringing events together in the order they happened, even though that is narration's basic organization. Have you ever listened to small children tell you about their day? First this happened, then that, then this, then that, and on and on. "Where is the story in the story?" you may ask. Telling a good story requires that there be a point to the story, one rooted in personal experience. The point is—you've got it— your discovered insight. The trip toward that insight dictates where you start and where you end your narration and how much time you spend on the events in-between.

The "write" question introduced in this chapter allows you to use your personal experience in a narration style essay to find insight. If you have no particular topic in mind, simply ask the question, "When have I lost (or found) something, someone, or some opportunity? You may remember things like losing your first job as a paperboy because someone invited you in for cookies and your cart rolled away or losing the chance to be High School Homecoming Queen because you were caught drinking. You may remember a friend you lost as you grew older or the piece of jewelry you lost in the back seat of a boy's car.

If you do have a topic you are exploring, insert it into the question. Using the example topics from Chapter Two, you could ask, "When in my divorce, parenting, illness, war experience, or visit to another country did I lose or find something, someone, or some opportunity? You might remember losing your home or a particular friend in a divorce. You might remember losing your way on a bicycle trip through the Netherlands and being rescued by a paraplegic with a ham radio. You might remember losing a fellow soldier, finding a ring on a battle ground, missing a chance to be stationed at a site that was bombed and finding yourself alive because of that. Losing and finding go hand-in-hand. When something is lost, something else is usually found and when something is found, something is usually lost. However, losing seems to have the most memories and feelings attached, and those feelings help you as a writer. Treasured coming-of-age stories seem to require that something is lost before maturity is gained. The personal essayist can discover moments of self-growth by writing narrations about loss and gain, of people, pets, relationships and opportunities.

Before I share the new exercise for gathering story material, let's turn to example essays that narrate times of loss.

Example Narration Essays

Author Steven Winn brought together the story of his father's last days with the story of taking his daughter to her first major league baseball game, where she catches a ball tossed by player Eric Karros. Notice how the essay moves chronologically through time and notice how more detail is given to some events than to others. Notice how the event of Winn's daughter opening a condolence note at the essay's end leads to its insight and resolution.

After the Ball

Earlier this spring, in the opening week of the new baseball season, my 10-year-old daughter and I attended our first game at Los Angeles' Dodger Stadium with a friend of ours. It was a charmed night, even for Giants fans venturing onto rival ground.

Our seats, by dumb luck, were right behind the Dodger dugout. Shawn Green and Paul Lo Duca chatted within earshot as we sat down. Adrian Beltre and Cesar Izturis played catch, ball-smacking leather in a lazy cadence. We could have counted the blades of grass at their feet.

My daughter, Phoebe, had a Dodger Dog and showed up on the DiamondVision screen eating it. An a cappella group sang the national anthem with fetching harmonies. Our friend Kurt, not much of a baseball enthusiast, amused himself shooting the field, late-arriving fans and glowing scoreboard with his digital camera. The game itself, against the Colorado Rockies, seemed like a bonus when it began.

In the second inning, something marvelous happened. After making a deft scoop for the last out, Dodger first baseman Eric Karros jogged for the dugout, paused an instant before stepping down and motioned to Phoebe with his glove. He rolled the ball across the dugout to her, a precious relic delivered directly from a player's hand. Even the blasé LA fans around us murmured their approving surprise.

Karros came up in the bottom of the inning with two men on and promptly sent a home run soaring toward the stadium's distinctive zigzag roofline in left field. Kurt and I grinned at the scripted perfection of it — the ball in the top of the inning, the home run in the bottom. For me it was pure father fantasy, my daughter and me caught up together in some sublime baseball destiny.

Phoebe, looking pleasantly dazed, wondered if we could share one of those blue plastic Dodger caps filled with french fries. We did. The Dodgers won — their first victory of the season. Karros wound up with three hits, two runs scored and three runs batted in for the night.

The next morning I phoned my father, who was recuperating from a nagging circulation problem in a rural Missouri hospital, and reported on the game. Never one for overt displays of enthusiasm, Dad sounded unusually energized by this news. He questioned me closely about what had happened and what Phoebe had made of it. When she got on the phone, he had her go over the whole story again.

Dad glossed over my own questions about his recovery — he was planning on going home that weekend — and asked me once more about the game, the treasured ball, the home run. "That's great," he said, with a practically audible grin. "That's just great."

Four days later I was back home in San Francisco, watching a Giants game on television and sorting 10 days' worth of mail, when the call came from my sister. Our father had had a stroke. He'd been sent to a hospital in Kansas City. It didn't look good.

My sister arrived in Kansas City from Milwaukee the next morning. I made it from the Bay Area early that afternoon. The stroke had been massive. A new procedure had removed the clot, but the damage to our father's brain was comprehensive. Swelling, over the next few days, would probably blot out speech and consciousness and finally all vital functions.

That's how it went. We spent the next 25 hours at or near his bedside, listening for and exchanging signs of recognition, lobbying the nurses, shuttling relatives and visitors in and out of the ICU. Some day I may remember more clearly what it was I said to my father, or he to me while he still could, on his last day. For now those hours in the hospital are a vivid blur, a stream of silent images: my father's face glazed in spring sunshine from the window, the colored lines cresting and falling on the monitor above his head, my mother's deep bedside gaze, a crow pecking at a pebbled rooftop outside.

And then, suddenly, we were planning a funeral, receiving guests and sympathy and casseroles. Sorrow, enormous as it seemed, left room for family gossip, anger, outbursts of hilarity and reminiscence. Several people mentioned the baseball game to me, and how much Dad had talked about it in those few days before his stroke. It appeared, from their accounting of it, that he might not have gotten or repeated the details quite right (he'd always cared more about football than baseball). But I was glad he'd been entertained by our adventure.

Two weeks after Dad died, Phoebe received a condolence letter from one of my parents' oldest friends. "The last time I talked with your grandfather," Mr. Mentzer wrote from Pennsylvania, "he told me about attending your first baseball game with your father. And how one of the players talked with you and asked what he could do for you. And how you asked him to hit a home run. And how he did — and gave you the ball!"

Everything about that description is so fabulously wrong that it sheds a kind of wondrous grace. The workaday player Eric Karros, in this modern myth, holds powers greater than those Babe Ruth tapped in calling his fabled home run in the 1932 World Series. My father would have been 15 years old at the time. He must have marveled, as a small-town Missouri teenager, over Ruth's putative "Shot Heard 'Round the World."

It delights me to think that, 70 years later, Dad spun a tale even more fantastical than Ruth's out of an early-season Dodgers-Rockies game attended by his son and granddaughter. Or maybe Mr. Mentzer and others unconsciously enlarged, in his honor, on my father's fond misapprehensions. Wild and fanciful exaggeration wasn't at all like my father. Or maybe, in the end, it was.

It's one of too many things to count that I'll never know. I can revisit the photographs Kurt e-mailed us after the game. I can follow the fortunes of Karros in the box scores, as Phoebe and I now faithfully do. A player on the downside of his career, he was hitting a very respectable .308 last week. I can go back to Dodger Stadium or Pac Bell Park and wait for something amazing to occur again.

But whatever happens, from now on, I'll have to tell the story myself.

How the Writer Makes a Discovery and Shares It in "After the Ball"

Steven Winn describes the game he takes his daughter to along with a friend. Time slows down during that description—we are at the game, immersed in the sounds, sights, and goings on. After that, the essay speeds up, covering more time with a few well-chosen details: first the contents of a phone call made to the author's father, then the contents of a call from his sister, then hours at the hospital and days planning a funeral, and then weeks until the condolence letter arrives. With the condolence note, the essayist slows down again in the telling. We learn what the letter says, and we learn how the author revels in the changes his father made to the baseball story. We learn how the writer feels he might cope in the coming days—viewing the pictures, following the player's scores, revisiting the stadium. In the list, details tie the essay's end back to its beginning, and in doing so, help the writer find his way to this important statement: "But whatever happens, from now on, I'll have to tell the story myself." Here is where the gain, the something found, comes in. Narrating this story, telling of its importance to his father and about the way his father's friend described it, Winn makes a realization—his stories will no longer be directed to his father. His father will no longer change the stories. Winn has moved up one generation. For Winn, stating this is the first step toward absorbing the impact of this life passage.

When you draft your narration essay, you may not know how much "time" to spend on each part of the story. However, after you read your first versions to a person or a writing group and find out how they felt following the story, you will be able to adjust your narration if the sequence or importance of events is not quite tuned up.

Here's another narration essay to sample, "Eating Pizza With Stacy" by Bora Lee Reed. In this essay, the author may be answering the "write question" with a thought like this one: I lost my friend Stacy to cancer. In her essay, she recounts a day not too long before her friend died. As the essay ends, the writer has drawn a memory of Stacy so vivid that she continues to live in spirit.

Eating Pizza With Stacy

Stacy is twenty-four years old and an athlete, but she moves like an old woman, unable to lift her feet and shuffling from bed to toilet to couch. She is dressed in what has become her uniform of the last six months: flannel pajama pants, t-shirt, knit cap, and fleece slippers.

I can tell that she is not displeased to see me, but she does not smile until her eyes settle on Anna.

"Wow," she says. She gestures with her hand, as though she is about to stroke Anna's head, then seems to decide against it and pulls back. "Wow," she repeats. "Cute."

In better days, Stacy and I would have taken Anna to the park. We would have felt the warmth of this day, and sat on a bench to watch little boys in striped shirts circle their bikes around the sandy playground. Stacy would have given me the latest update on her beloved Giants; I would have feigned interest and she would have responded kindly to my ignorance. A poorly thrown Frisbee might come sailing toward us. Stacy would pick it up and deftly return it, the leanness of her tan arm in dark relief against her white t-shirt.

Today is not that kind of day.

For lunch we decide to order in because Stacy's legs hurt too much for her to go out. I call for a pizza, insisting on a large despite Stacy's protests.

"There's no way I can eat a large pizza," she says.

Still, I feel the need to counter the quiet grayness of the room. The cold linoleum floors, the kitchen that has gone unused for months, the lingering disinfectant smell and the muted sadness between us has diminished any sign of spring. I want to do something brash and extravagant. For now, a pizza will do.

"We can put the leftovers in the fridge. You can eat it tomorrow." Tomorrow. Tomorrow. The thought comforts me.

The pizza arrives. It is, of course, too much. We sit on her faded brown couch, the greasy wheel of cheese and pepperoni between us. Stacey eats like she does everything else - slowly, with determination. Her brows — or at least the place on her face where her brows used to be — furrow in concentration as she lifts a piece to her mouth. She chews slowly, wiping her pale lips after every bite with a paper napkin. It takes her ten long minutes to work her way through half of one slice.

Meanwhile, Anna has gotten hungry. She squirms and moves her head from side to side-mouth agape, looking for milk. Her cry sounds alarmingly loud. For a moment our attention shifts to the baby; it is a relief to have something else to focus on.

"Does it hurt?" asks Stacy suddenly. "Does what hurt?"

"Childbirth, breastfeeding, all that stuff. It all seems so painful."

Stacy has endured catheters being burrowed into an artery in her chest. She has watched her dark, chestnut hair fall out in clumps - on the pillow, in the shower, on her mother's shoulder. She has stared down a hospital bed at her belly, distended from infection. She has lost dangerous amounts of weight; she is a wisp of her former self. For weeks at a time, she has been so weakened that she could barely speak, only raising her head when she needed to vomit, sometime a dozen times a day. And she has endured the worst of all. After all the suffering, the cure that was almost worse than the disease, the hours of prayer and holding onto hope, she has received the news she has dreaded most: the cancer is back.

"Childbirth hurts," I finally reply. "But it's nothing like cancer."

The afternoon is meandering along; the sun has slipped a degree lower and dappled shadows play across our faces.

"Can I hold the baby?"

Anna has eaten and lies contently, passed out in a haze of a milk-induced stupor. Stacy reaches out and I gingerly place my child in her bony arms. Weighing less than ten pounds, Anna looks heavy cradled there. Stacy peers into Anna's sleeping face: the dying holding the newly born. It is terrible and wonderful.

Today is Friday, May 12. Next Wednesday, Stacy will die. I will stand near the back of the room and watch her family mourn her lifeless body. I will notice that Stacy died on her side, curled up in a fetal position. Her mother will cry silently, stroking her hand. Kind people will encourage me to say "good-bye." I will approach and reach out and touch Stacy's heel with the tips of my fingers. Her foot will still be warm.

I will spend my days taking long walks. Images of Stacy's last months will play through my mind like a series of film shorts: Stacy at Thanksgiving eating turkey in the hospital; Stacy enduring chemo, barely alive; Stacy cheering the San Francisco Giants; Stacy smiling, showing all her teeth. I will be surprised that mourning feels like a stomachache. I will resist the urge to slap people whose lives move along, cheerful and uninterrupted. I will be numb. I will wonder if I did all that I could. I will worry about how Stacy's mother is doing. I will fear burying my own child someday.

Much later, I will be ready to talk about Stacy with my children. I will say, "Stacy was our friend. She was kind and brave and full of faith. She loved to tell people about Jesus. She had leukemia. We hoped she would live, but she died. We miss her."

But not today. All that is in our future — in my future. For this afternoon, there is only Stacy holding Anna, a mostly uneaten pizza, and me.

"How am I doing?" Stacy wants to know.

A breeze stirs the trees outside. I get up and close the window to keep out the chill.

"You're a natural, Stacy," I say. "You two look great together."

And they did.

How the Writer Makes a Discovery and Shares It in "Eating Pizza with Stacy"

When we lose someone close to us, we may want to recapture this person in our writing. Reed's essay recounts a day toward the end of her ill friend's life as well as the day she died, and it memorializes the friend's spirit and connection to life. The story of taking her infant daughter, Anna, to visit Stacy allows the author to recount the way Stacy focused on life by asking about childbirth and wanting to hold the baby. As Stacy holds the baby, our author writes about the future, less than a week from this day, when Stacy will die. She talks about saying goodbye, about her thoughts after the death and the fears she may hold all her life. Then Reed relates how she will be ready some day to talk about Stacy. She will remember the moment Stacy held Anna and said, "How am I doing?" As the author went to close the window to keep out a chill, both real and emotional, she said, "You're a natural, Stacy," and meant it.

The narration of the time she lost her friend begins with the last visit to her when she was alive, travels to her death, and then returns to the last visit because that is the current memory. The essay captures life, though it be waning, and we feel both joy and deep sadness.

Locating Your Narration Material

Answer the "write" question for narration by clustering your thoughts about "What times do I remember when I lost or found something, someone, or some opportunity?" or "What times do I remember while _____ (for example again, getting divorced, becoming a parent, adjusting to an illness, fighting a war, visiting another country) that I lost or found something, someone, or some opportunity?" This time, put the words "lost and found," or just the word "lost" or just the word "found," in the center of a piece of paper. Draw a circle around the word or words you wrote. Let yourself free associate to times that go with the words in your mind and write them down on the page, circling them and connecting the circles to the center circle. If you think of more details to go with each memory, make new clusters around the memories. Don't censor yourself. Just jot down more memories and more details you remember. Circle each phrase or detail you write. Use lines to connect the circles that cluster together.

Chose one of the memories you thought of and about which you made a cluster and do a freewrite about it for 10 minutes. Try to recount the events that led up to the loss or the find in the order that they happened. Put your freewrite away for now.

Just like with the description essay, you will have put yourself on the trail of material from your life experience, whether it was losing money your parents had given you or being with a dying relative or friend or pet. You might have thought of a time you lost a part in a play or remembered finding a precious object or a new friend or an unexpected chance to travel. Don't worry about how to organize the narration just yet.

Instead, do the "This is a Poem" exercise or the analogy exercise from the description essay chapter. These can be helpful in developing material for a narration essay, especially since, as you have seen, many of the events in the sequence must be aptly described.

There is one more poetry exercise that can help you collect information about the event you are writing about.

This exercise is modeled after Gary Synder's poem, "Things to Do Around a Lookout." In his poem, Synder lists things to do while he is spending time as a lookout for the National Forest Service. He talks about wrapping up in a blanket to read, practicing writing

Chinese characters, baking coffee cake, hunting firewood, and drinking lapsang soochong tea among other activities. In his poem, Synder describes each of his activities in detail. Rice is put out, not for animals in general, but for "the ptarmigan and the conies."

Think about what you have decided to write about and title a piece "Things that Happened When I Lost/Found _____". Make as long of a list of things that happened as you can. Then try this exercise again entitling it, "Things That I Didn't Do When I Lost/ Found _____". In this way, you might come up with details that allow you to see how different the time you are writing about was from other times.

Writing Your Essay

After you have done the exercises, look again at the example essays in this chapter to note how they begin. "After the Ball" tells us the time and place of the first event of the series: earlier this spring at Los Angeles Dodger Stadium. In "Eating Pizza With Stacy," the author opens by telling her readers where she is standing. She knocks and hears her friend say to come in.

Langston Hughes, a famous African-American writer from the Midwest, who became part of the Harlem Renaissance in the thirties, started "Salvation," a narrative chapter in his autobiography, *The Big Sea* (1940) with these three sentences: "I was saved from sin when I was going on thirteen. But not really saved. It happened like this." Hughes goes on in his first paragraph to give a synopsis of a big revival that had been going on at his aunt's church for weeks. He tells how excitement was building for a special meeting for children. And he ends his paragraph with the sentence that focuses the story he will tell: "That night, I was escorted to the front row and placed on the mourner's bench with all other young sinners, who had not yet been brought to Jesus." We are about to learn the events of that night and the outcome in terms of what he lost and what he gained as he sat and waited for the moment of his salvation.

Now try your hand at a draft of your narration essay. You might want to start with a description of where you stand as your story starts or with a sentence like, "This is a story about the time I . . . ," or "Usually things went like _____ for me, but this time something else happened." Write from what seems to be the beginning of the story to what seems to be the end. Even when your essay is not fully developed, you can feel where you are entering interesting territory by the rise in your level of your attention and the flood of details returning to you. Trust this.

Keep Drafting

Review the three-step response method described in Chapter III. Have your trusted readers give you their response or use the response method yourself on your draft. As you write, re-write and receive response, you will get in touch with what you learned from the event you are narrating and discover why you are telling the story you have chosen to tell. It is not that you must state directly what you learned. Rather, what you learned becomes the real story, and the details you choose and the events you describe serve that story.

Chapter V

The How-To Essay

Write Question #3: What do I know how to make or do?

> *. . . there is the mnemonic potential of language—the capacity to use this tool to help one remember information, ranging from lists of possessions to rules of a game, from directions for finding one's way to procedures for operating a new machine.*
>
> > —Howard Gardner
> > *Frames of Mind:*
> > *The Theory of Multiple Intelligences*

*I*n our culture, we are very familiar with the how-to style of writing. It is not hard to find how-to books and articles on subjects as wide ranging as making a marriage work, becoming a super learner or performer, wiring a house, lowering cholesterol, and preparing for alien abduction. All of us read about how to do things and/or make products.

In getting an education, pursuing hobbies, raising families, and doing jobs, we learn how things are made and how they work. Some of us know first-hand how a particular government agency works, how landing gear on an airplane works, how to make yogurt or paper or a web site. Some of us are able to juggle two jobs while raising a family; others know something about how to resolve conflict successfully or how to play badminton. But why would we write about how to do these things in a personal essay?

When you write a personal essay using the how-to form, you often write about how something is done or made to address *particular people you care about or disagree with*. There is something in the process you are writing about that you want them to appreciate or see as a metaphor for a life situation or understand to be better informed. You want your audience to understand how the process of making or doing a particular thing has affected your life and could affect theirs.

Some of the most moving how-to essays I've read explain step-by-step how to do something that the authors actually wished they didn't really know how to do. These topics include how to become co-dependent, lose hard-earned savings, alienate a spouse, lose a child's respect, have practically no friends, and take actions that will ruin the environment. Authors of the how-to personal essay can write to help those they care about avoid doing what they have done.

All how-to writing requires paying attention to 1) the steps in the process you are describing, 2) the order in which the steps must be performed, 3) the special terms to understand 4) the tools required to do the process, 5) the variations allowed in approaches, and 6) the signs that the desired outcome has been achieved. This organization contains sequence much like narration contains chronology. It contains description as you write about stages in a process and involves the five senses as you make the process immediate for the reader. In addition, the how-to essay can contain anecdotes (short narrations) as a way of describing any of the steps. How-to personal essays also make clear to the reader why the author is explaining how a particular thing is made or done.

Because I think the how-to form of the personal essay is intended for particular people in an author's life, I suggest borrowing from the epistolary or letter form of writing to focus the how-to personal essay. By thinking of both something you know how to do or make and someone you believe needs this information, you will be ready to write an effective how-to personal essay.

If you intend to write about an area of experience you have already decided to explore, ask yourself the "write" question like this: What do I know how to do or to make concerning _____ (for example once again, divorce, parenting, adjusting to an illness, fighting in a war or visiting another country)? To whom do I most want to tell this? Your answer to the first question might range from how to file for divorce and how to work out joint custody to how to make divorce harder on yourself and everyone you love. When you think about to whom you want to tell the information, you will narrow down possible topics. Perhaps you'll find the topic that most appeals is the one about joint custody, addressed to your children so their new life is easier for them. Or perhaps you want to address your ex-husband on the topic to make a point about how important it is that children's lives continue with as little interruption as possible.

After you figure out whom you want to address, you might find yourself rearranging the topic a little. Maybe you see that you want to write to your ex-husband about the need for joint custody and you realize the most effective way to do this is to write about how to wreck joint custody and the kids' emotional lives, too.

If you are not thinking about a particular topic for your writing, ask, "What do I know how to do or to make? Who do I most want to tell this to?"

Whether you have already decided on a particular interest or not, do two clusters. In the first one, put "how is made or done" in the middle of the page and circle and connect whatever words come to mind, whether you are clustering on one particular process or fishing around for one of interest. You might find yourself thinking about how to make your grandmother's rhubarb pie, how to cheer up a toddler, how to mess up a house, how to earn points with the boss, how to find a new friend, or how to care for a sick friend. You will be surprised at what you can explain to someone else. Next, cluster around the phrase, "To whom do I want to tell something?"

Pretty soon, you will think of some surprising people, or even inanimate objects, you might want to write a how-to personal essay for—a former teacher, a dead relative, a close friend, the annoying business associate at the next desk, your favorite stuffed animal from childhood, your mother, father, spouse, lover or children.

After asking the questions and answering them with the help of clustering, you will find topics and audiences you are interested in. Choose one topic and audience. Then do image-gathering exercises for the topic you have chosen using the "Things to Do" and "This is a Poem" strategies. Later, I will introduce a new exercise for gathering how-to material for your essay. First let's look at two sample how-to essays to see how they work.

Example How-to Essays

In "Letter to My Friend John," Tim Johnson describes the process of planting and raising a pinto bean harvest. Johnson feels he can connect to his friend on this subject because he has already told him that he brought pinto beans home from his annual trip to North Dakota. By describing the process of pinto bean farming, Johnson realizes that what he is describing is also a metaphor for how his friend has recovered in the years following his wife's murder. There are steps to growing the beans and steps to rebuilding a life. To communicate the processes clearly, Johnson uses description and narration.

Letter to My Friend John

Dear John

I value our friendship too much to want to dredge up past memories that are too painful for you to relive. During the past eight years, standing by you through your painful journey, I never asked to talk about anything you didn't want to share, but I want to tell you how much I admire you. The best way I know to describe my understanding of your courage is through an analogy.

When I brought some pinto beans home last fall upon my return from my annual harvest pilgrimage to North Dakota, I told you that it was the first time that pinto beans were raised on my land. After cleaning out the field dirt, rinsing and soaking the beans, I prepared them in a slow cooker. One of the recipes I concocted is with *hefeweitzen* or wheat beer, a ham bone and various seasonings including Worcestershire sauce. It makes for some fine eating!

I renegotiated my farm leasing arrangement with the cousin who planted the bean crop last year. The deal I struck with Gary will include a cash rent-share crop arrangement. He will pay me cash rent on all the tillable crop acres except for the pinto bean acres. On those acres, we will share an 80-20 split of the crop. In other words, I will get 20 percent of the production as the landlord. I made this arrangement with him because pinto beans are an intensive high input crop, and there are many risks associated with raising them.

I will share the risks because I want Gary to raise pinto beans. I want to break out of the cereal crop rotation, which has left the overall soil fertility, especially nitrogen, at low levels. As you know pinto beans are a legume so they will fix atmospheric nitrogen in the soil thereby cutting down on the need and expense of using only commercial fertilizer. Weed control is a very important step in raising a successful crop of pinto beans. Gary will use various herbicides in this step but will also do mechanical cultivation. While cultivating, he also marks the surface rocks that he can see with small red flags. However, the main reason for cultivation is to "hill" the rows.

"Hilling" is important because it throws dirt into the rows. Harvesting is a three-step process that involves first knifing or under cutting the roots and bunching two rows together. The hilling process created by cultivation allows the four-foot long knives to work properly and is mainly done at night when the bean vines are damp with dew. The damp vines flow over the knives in a smoother motion. When the vines dry out they start to bunch up. Seeing the red flags that mark the surface rocks allows the operator of the knifer to lift over the rocks so that the knife assembly isn't damaged any more than necessary. One pass with the knifing apparatus is usually not enough to sever all the roots, so he also has to make a pass with a rotating rod assembly that runs underground and loosens the remaining roots. The last harvest step is threshing the bunched rows with a combine that is modified for this operation. The combine is equipped with a special header that eliminates some of the small rocks and dirt picked up with the beans. The rotary cylinder is slowed down so as not to crack and split the beans during the threshing process. Splits are part of the dockage that includes other dirt and are discounted when unloaded at the transfer elevator. Once the beans are unloaded from the collection hopper of the combine, they can be used immediately.

In relating how Gary raises a crop of pinto beans, I am especially thinking about the challenges in your personal life during the last eight years. Just as my soil suffered depletion of life-giving nitrogen, your life lost its sustenance following Marta's death. Instead of giving up, though, you chose to help renew the soil with a pilgrimage back to Paraguay to return Marta's ashes to her family and attend the nine-day novena, which though difficult, helped you and your son with closure. You eliminated weeds in your life by testifying at the trial of Marta's assailant and then cultivated the future by bringing a lawsuit against the entities and the system, which allowed him to prey upon women in this city. By doing so, you created a future for Tom.

When you met Anna, perhaps you didn't realize that she would figure into your life within a few years. But while you were cultivating the future, you also "hilled" the rows of your life by striking up a correspondence with her and having visits in which you got to know her daughter Diana and she Tom. The harvest process in your relationship began with your wedding almost four years ago. Following the wedding, she severed the roots of her old life and moved to Tucson to be with you, but there have been rocks in the rows, which you have had to lift over. The readjustment process for all of you has been the bunching of the rows of your individual lives. Not all the roots have been severed by just one pass and the process of threshing out the vines of diversity and expectations hasn't always been easy.

You more than anyone knows that life doesn't come with guarantees or without risk. Eight years ago, 100 percent of your life was at risk. Slowly but surely you have been able to turn around the situation from that of an operator who assumes all the risks to that of a landlord, willing to risk 20 percent in order to be a better steward. The benefits have been great. The cleaning and separation of the fruits of your lives still has its share of splits and dockage. However, you are now cooking the soup together with Anna and Tom and Diana, with the fruit of all your efforts, and adding seasonings, making for some pretty good sustenance.

Please accept my words and admiration.

Sincerely yours,

Tim

How the Writer Makes a Discovery and Shares It in "Letter to My Friend John"

Notice that to organize parts of the how-to essay, Tim Johnson used various forms of rhetoric inside the main organizational plan. He delineates the steps from legal arrangements to cultivating the soil, planting and harvesting the beans. His descriptions provide precise images and details. Anecdotes help demonstrate and set scenes of the process under discussion. Johnson defines technical terms and tells us the effects of doing certain steps improperly. Once he has done this, he turns from describing the process in farming to applying the process to his friend's personal recovery. Here he uses metaphor and comparison and contrast-style thinking (which we will work with more in the next chapter) to evoke his feelings and ideas.

❧

Although the letter form helps you to encounter and use deeply emotional material, you will not always require it when writing about processes. Here is an essay that describes how the words on the Statue of Liberty got to be there.

The Lighted Lamp of Emma Lazarus

Buried in the history of the Statue of Liberty is the story of a woman named Emma Lazarus. She is part of the history because of her authorship of these words: "Give me your tired, your poor, Your huddled masses yearning to breathe free. The wretched refuse of your teeming shore. Send these, the homeless, tempest-tost to me, I lift my lamp beside the golden door!"

Just who was Emma Lazarus, and how did her sonnet, "The New Colossus," come to be part of the monument and change its meaning?

Emma was an American Jew, born in New York City in 1849, who grew up privileged and sheltered. She knew little of poverty, slavery or anti-Semitism. What she did know was poetry, the classics and the works of the transcendentalists.

Emma's early poems, melodramatic adolescent musings, were privately printed by her devoted father for family members. But her first volume also found its way into the hands of one of her idols, Ralph Waldo Emerson, who, on meeting her, kindly offered to read her work and gave her his address in Concord. This began a long correspondence, and Emerson, who guided many a literary aspirant, added young Emma to his list of protégées.

After years of friendship, though, he abandoned her, leaving the reclusive Emma, now approaching her 30s, seriously reflecting on her life's purpose. A literary friend suggested that there was a wealth in her Jewish heritage. She responded that, while she was proud of her religion and ancestry, she considered herself more an American than a Jew. Events in Russia changed that view. The year

1881 saw a new rage of anti-Semitism so violent that the world had trouble comprehending it. In city after city Cossack soldiers destroyed Jewish districts, burning homes and synagogues, murdering and terrifying the people.

Jews by the thousands set sail for America. An acquaintance of Emma who was active in the Hebrew Emigrant Aid Society brought a group of women, including Emma, to visit the temporary housing facility, Ward's Island, to see "the wretched fugitives . . . the victims of Russian barbarity."

The refined, sheltered Emma was shocked and profoundly moved by what she saw. Immediately she threw herself into helping the refugees. She overcame her shyness to arrange meetings that led to the establishment of a trade school for boys. But her real strength was in the power of her pen. She became a regular contributor to newspapers and periodicals, writing not only impassioned poetry but strong editorials and controversial letters as well.

For two years she worked hard and then traveled abroad for the first time. On her return to New York, she found glamor and confusion over the building of a pedestal in New York Harbor.

France was about to present America with a statue called "Liberty Enlightening the World," and America was to provide the pedestal. Publisher Joseph Pulitzer raised the country's conscience with a relentless fund-raising campaign in his newspapers. The final sum necessary to complete the pedestal came from an auction of literary works by luminaries including Mark Twain, Walt Whitman, and John Burroughs.

Emma Lazarus was approached to contribute a poem. She thought of the Colossus of Rhodes, a huge bronze statue of the sun god Helios, built in an Aegean harbor in ancient times. Now America would have a monument at its gateway that would welcome all people. She wrote "The New Colossus." The portfolio went to the highest bidder for $1,500.

In October, 1886, the statue was dedicated, but Emma was not at the ceremony. She was gravely ill with cancer. She died Nov. 19, 1887, at the age of 38.

Her sonnet was not forgotten, thanks to Georgina Schuyler, a patroness of the arts. One day in 1903 she was browsing in a used-book store and came across a dusty portfolio. A sonnet, "The New Colossus," in which the poet called the statue the "Mother of Exiles," struck her as a verse that would add lasting meaning to the monument. She arranged for the last five lines to be inscribed on a plaque and hung inside the pedestal. On that ordinary day, with no fanfare, Frederic Auguste Bartholdi's sculpture and Emma Lazarus' inspired words were united, together a monument that continues to stir us all.

How the Writer Makes a Discovery and Shares It in "The Lighted Lamp of Emma Lazarus"

"Just who was Emma Lazarus, and how did her sonnet, 'The New Colossus,' come to be part of the monument and change its meaning?" How many of us know the famous words on the Statue of Liberty but never thought about where they were from? Here Nancy Smiler Levinson makes use of the how-to essay to let us know how the words were created and the way they came to be inscribed on the monument. Although she researched this information before she started to write, the information comes as a discovery to the reader. To answer the question she poses for us, Levinson needs to show us who Emma Lazarus was, what she wrote, her connection to the Statue of Liberty, and the actual liaison who connected those words to the monument. There is an order here that must be followed if the story is going to make sense. The delivery of the information uses the style of narration along with the steps of how-to to show how the words on the statue came to be inscribed. The researched details allow us to see the process, and we also learn that it was Lazarus' lines that spun the meaning of the statue toward a welcoming of immigrants. The reader, like the researcher, discovers that the statue was meant as a commemoration of liberty and not as a celebration of immigration. That the statue became synonymous with the American Dream and melting pot is because of these words: "Give me your tired, your poor, Your huddled masses yearning to breathe free. The wretched refuse of your teeming shore. Send these, the homeless, tempest-tost to me, I lift my lamp beside the golden door!"

Exercises for Developing Your Material

Although you may feel familiar with description and narration as writing styles, you may feel unsure about your skill in using other organizational patterns, such as how-to. However, even if you haven't been using patterns other than description and narration in writing, you have been using them in your lives. In this and following chapters, I share exercises that help you connect with your experience using these patterns.

To grease the wheels of your "how-to" thinking try this one:

The If-I-Can-Do-It-I-Can-Help-You-Understand-How-to-Do-It-Too Exercise

Find someone to interview about something he or she knows how to do, someone who is also willing to interview you about something you know how to do. For example, suppose you have an acquaintance who knows how to develop film, or use public transportation efficiently, or prepare soil for vegetable gardening. Bring a pen and pad and ask your interviewee to tell you why the particular task is important to him or her. Jot down the reason. Ask why it is important for others to know how to do the task. Jot this down, too. Next, ask your interviewee to describe the steps, one by one, performed in doing the task. Take notes. If the steps don't make sense to you, ask questions until you have all the terms and procedures straight and you understand what is done in what order and how to do each part of the process.

Referring to your notes, tell the process back to your interviewee. Does he or she think you got it right? If not, you probably need a further description or a different order to the steps given you. Let your interviewee help until you are both satisfied that you could perform the task using his or her directions.

Now that you have experienced *receiving* how-to information, switch roles. Have your interviewee become your interviewer. With pad and pen for taking notes, your interviewer will now ask you about something you know how to do and listen to you tell why someone else might want to know how to do it. Perhaps you will discuss how to stop smoking, or how to unplug a toilet, or how to create a savings plan that works. Whatever your subject, have your interviewer ask you to tell the steps needed to accomplish the task, one by one, in the right order. Your interviewer should ask questions to clarify any special terms, tools, materials, variations, or precautions necessary for the task. After the interview is completed, let your interviewer describe your process back to you. Would he or she be doing it right the way they are telling it to you? If not, what do you need to do—correct a step, add steps, or give more information?

Anytime you have given someone travel directions or shared a recipe, you have communicated in the how-to style. Anytime you have tried to assemble something from manufacturers' directions or used a product according to instructions, you have experienced receiving information in the how-to style. You know how important clarity, precision, correct order, and pertinent information are for the receiver! Whenever you are using the how-to form, whether it is to teach family members how to do Thanksgiving the way your grandparents did it or to tell your best friend how to overcome the grief of an unwanted divorce, that same thoroughness will create essays that are rich, full, and well received.

Locating Your How-to Material

Now that you have practiced noticing the steps in a process, look back at your clusters and the image-gathering exercises you did on your topic. With these in front of you, do a freewrite in which you take on the task of revealing how something is done, or made, or came to be. Remember your audience. Write continuously for five to twenty minutes describing how something is made or done for the benefit of that audience. When the time is up, shake out your hands and do something besides rereading the freewrite.

Writing Your Essay

When you have spent some time away from the freewrite, sit down again and look at it. Write a short account of a time you remember sharing something with the person to whom you are writing, or contemplate a future time for which you want to prepare this person. After grounding your reader in a situation, state the process you want him or her to understand. Then describe the steps that need to be done for the process to be completed. Take care to get the order right and not to leave any important steps out. Pay attention to your use of description and terms in the steps. Are the images sensory and true to the situation? Do any of the terms need explanation? How will the reader know when he or she has accomplished the process? If you concentrate on answering these questions as you describe the steps, you will evoke more and more of your subject and keep your reader involved.

If you get stuck describing any of the steps, stop and do a cluster or a "This is a Poem" or a "Things to Do" exercise for that step. You will create images that help you get unstuck.

Now, consider a sentence from Latin American writer Eduardo Galeano in his book, *Days and Nights of Love and War* (Monthly Review Press, 1983): "I believe in my vocation; I believe in my instrument." If the idea of telling a story about a shared time to start your how-to essay doesn't appeal to you, use Galeano's words as a prompt. Fill in the vocation involved in your how-to. Let the reader know what you believe in.

Keep Drafting

Once again, get response to your draft or go through the three steps yourself. Then get back to your draft with the responses you received. Let yourself write more from beginning to end. Can a reader both *follow your steps* and *feel why* you are really addressing them about how something is made or done? Gather new responses to your continuing drafts and develop your work until you feel satisfied.

Chapter VI

The Comparison and Contrast Essay

Write Question #4: What in my life is not the way it is supposed to be?

> World is the pattern of meaningful relations in which a person exists and in the design of which he or she participates.
> —Rollo May, *The Courage to Create*

We use comparison and contrast to make choices—between jobs, consumer goods, vacations, and equipment. We examine similarities and differences. We compare an unknown to something with which we are already familiar. We also use comparison and contrast to learn about ourselves. One person might learn more about his or her attachment to a hot rod by comparing it to having a celebrity in the neighborhood. Another might learn more about why he or she likes swimming in a pool better than swimming in the ocean by discussing the differences between the pool and the ocean in accessibility, temperature, and depth. Yet another might compare and contrast both kinds of swimming and find characteristics that make each a favorite way to swim.

We also use comparison and contrast to write personal essays that lead to self-discovery. I developed a "write" question for using this essay style from a statement made by a friend who had recently returned to the U.S. after living in Morocco. He had felt the magic of living in Morocco and not in America, where, he said, our need to pay bills forces us into making a living rather than living. He said sorrowfully, "It's not the way it's supposed to be." He had found something important to him in his life in Morocco that he didn't feel he had in his United States life. Our discussion made me think about the way most of us compare how we are living to how others (or internalized others) think we should. I rushed off to teach a class, with the phrase still in my head. I used it with my students to develop comparison/contrast essays from their personal experience.

I urged my students to use the phrase to compare and contrast the way they were living to how they or others close to them would wish them to live. I wanted them to explore ways in which their lives were both like and unlike what they or someone else might wish them to be.

We think we know what other people want or expect from us, and we contrast what we are doing with those expectations. Often, we feel we are doing less than what we are "supposed" to be doing. But what if we stop for a moment and examine our lives using the comparison and contrast style of essay writing?

To try this: Ask, "In my life, what is not the way it's supposed to be?" You will see how the question opens up new areas for writing and thinking and how it allows things to come to mind that contrast with the way you or someone else thought "it" would be. Are you a teacher instead of a doctor? Single instead of married? Living on a farm instead of in a city? Adopting children instead of having them? Living far away from family instead of close by? Baking your own bread instead of buying it?

You might start thinking of how you selected a career or a boyfriend and defied your parents' expectations, or how you worked a job because the money was good but discovered you wanted something quite different. You might compare what you think are the rights of all children to what has actually happened to children you know or to yourself as a child. What things in your life "are not the way they are supposed to be"?

If you have a subject in mind, insert it into the write question. To use our examples once again: "What about divorcing, parenting, adjusting to an illness, fighting a war, or visiting a new country is not the way it's supposed to be?" Your parenting style might contrast with how you hoped you'd parent. Your life with diabetes is different from your life before you had it. Actual battle experiences differ from imagined battles. We are all different from the norm, from an idealized version of life, from our old selves, and from those who came before us. Here is an opportunity to examine the differences and see what you have gained or what is missing for you.

Let's turn to two sample essays and see how they are organized and how their authors accomplish self-discovery. Note how the authors use descriptive, narrative, and instructive elements that we covered in earlier chapters.

Comparison and Contrast Essays to Sample

"Softball" by Susan Hagen describes the time when she longed to play softball in her town's summer kids league, but was not allowed to by her parents, who thought playing softball would jeopardize the orthodontic work on her mouth. Her life was not as she hoped it would be. When she turned 32, however, she found the camaradrie and fun she had always longed for. Now her life was the way she wanted it to be, but not the way her mother would have had it.

Softball

The braces on my teeth were the reason my parents said no to girls' summer softball. Never mind that there wasn't much else to do in our rural valley town while the sun was busy killing off all the grass. Never mind that summer was softball, or how badly I needed to belong. "That's my fur coat you're wearing on your teeth," my mother said. "That's my trip to Hawaii for the next ten years. I won't have it be all for naught."

So I didn't beg to play, and I didn't ask again. Instead, I became a lone figure circling the playing fields on my cousin's outgrown bike, the silver in my mouth weighing me down like a debt I'd never be able to repay.

Late afternoons I rolled my bike down the driveway and began my rounds behind the backstops of forbidden softball worlds, steering a crooked path over chalky beds of broken eucalyptus and bricks of hardened earth. Past the pop-up fouls and sprained fingers of the fifth and sixth graders. Beyond the line drives and sifting grit of junior high girls sliding into the bags. Around the wide perimeters of the high school, where older girls stretched silk-screened shirts across stiff new bras and wore cut-offs trimmed to the water line.

Everywhere I rode were the sounds of me being left out. Even from the silent covered walkways of the primary school I could hear the children I'd known since kindergarten growing up without me. I skimmed past the windowed doors of my first and second grade classrooms, looped around the monkey bars, crisscrossed the buckled asphalt playground where I'd learned to play jacks and shoot marbles with these same girls. I practiced the slalom around naked stands of tetherball poles, traced the foul lines for dodge ball and foursquare with my wide balloon tires. Time had moved me beyond these innocent games of the past, and I was exiled from all relevant contests of the present. Because I couldn't lay claim to softball, I held no hope for a future inside those tight little knots of comrades whose lives intersected on the dying lawns of summer. I didn't belong to them. I didn't belong to anyone or anything but a self-sacrificing mother and a mouthful of costly orthodontia. I rode until the games were finished, the diamonds settled in dust. I rode my tires bald.

The summer I turned fifteen, the bands came off my teeth and I was fitted with a plastic retainer that clung to the roof of my mouth like hot grilled cheese. While the other girls were signing up for softball and oiling down their mitts, I applied for a job at the hamburger stand at the four-way stop in town. I had a work permit and a good reference from my school counselor, but what appealed to Floyd most about hiring me was that he wouldn't have to make my schedule around softball.

As the days fell away and evenings turned to dusk, I watched whole neighborhoods of kids spill out of station wagons and pick-up trucks to form ragged lines at my takeout window. They pushed and pulled at each other, picked at scabs on their elbows, and whether or not they'd won that night, threw their caps to the sky in a fountain of team color. Their energy broke through the portals of the Frostic like anxious bees breaching the screen to orbit the root beer taps. For that one hectic hour, I too, tasted the sweetness of softball, fielding orders for hot dogs and firing off chocolate-dipped cones as if I were pitching for the major leagues.

But then the rush was over, and I was left alone with a tired old man to flush out the ice cream machine and pick up the trash and chase sugar-sick insects with a dirty plastic flyswatter.

I was thirty-two years old before I played on a softball team, a women's league in San Francisco that promised "noncompetitive fun for inexperienced players." I borrowed a friend's mitt and bought a pair of canvas shoes with rubber cleats, took a bus to practice and worried about getting hit in the mouth.

The women on my team spit and swore, smoked cigarettes, iced down swollen knees with cold cans of Bud. They didn't care that I swung at the ball with my eyes closed, that I was afraid to get under a fly. Never mind that I stood in right field and wept like there was no bottom to my well of sorrow and joy. "A team is a team," they said. "We're glad you're here."

As we crowded into the coach's Toyota after our first big game, I burrowed into the warm tangle of arms and legs like a contented pup. A steamy mix of wet grass and women's sweat rose inside the car, brewing in the afterglow of softball. Someone popped the last

Bud and as it passed from hand to hand, I inhaled the tangy, fermented scent of a team that finally belonged to me. I ran my tongue along the edges of my mother's fur coat and tasted the beer on her tickets to Hawaii.

How the Author Makes a Discovery and Shares It in "Softball"

Susan Hagen plunges right into the essay with her mother's declaration that the braces she wore cost her parents money that would otherwise have bought fur coats and trips to Hawaii. Guilt ridden, the author did not participate in softball with friends. After the braces were replaced by a retainer, she signed up for a job rather than the softball team. Hagen describes herself alone, after the victorious team members celebrated at the Frostie where she worked "with a tired old man to flush out the ice cream machine and pick up the trash and chase sugar-sick insects with a dirty plastic fly-swatter." The images portray continued frustration and longing, and once Hagen mentions the "old man," she uses age to switch to her own adulthood: "I was thirty-two before I played on a softball team." Her life now contrasts to the time she spent as a loner not allowed to follow her passion. When we read about her 32-year-old self sipping a can of post-game beer with happy teammates, we instantly compare this scene to the one of the girl behind the counter at the Frostie. When she writes, "I ran my tongue along the edges of my mother's fur coat and tasted the beer on her tickets to Hawaii," we know she is comparing her happiness to the pleasures her mother said were denied because of the cost of braces. No longer guilty, she is happy with her life, though it is not as her mother would have liked it—softball instead of furs.

❧

In another comparison and contrast essay, "Feast of All Souls," Susan Bono compares her *berock*, a pastry filled with steamed cabbage and ground beef, to her grandmother's. The author's ability to make the dish is not, to her mind, as it should be, and she has been reluctant to try serving it. However, the day she tackles the recipe, she experiences a flood of memories.

Feast of All Soul's

For someone like me, a whole day in the kitchen requires more fortitude than I can usually muster, which is why I was feeling a little disoriented that Sunday evening in October. The last time I'd looked out the window, the afternoon was in full swing, but when I stepped outside to dump the garbage, the last of the thin sapphire light had nearly drained from the sky. Behind the scent of wood smoke and the promise of colder nights, I could smell the edges of the crinkling leaves and the aroma of a waxing moon, musty and sharp, like the inside of a split geode. I stood on the front porch, trying to make it all register. The night smelled like something I should remember forever, but probably wouldn't, no matter how hard I tried.

I must have sighed just before I stepped into our carpeted entry, expecting my next breath to catch on the familiar odors of steamed broccoli, dust and teenaged boys. Instead, I inhaled the scent of another place and time. Suddenly, I could have been a small child bursting eagerly into my grandparents' living room, darting around the legs of my uncles and aunts, drawn by the intoxicating fragrance of cooked cabbage, hamburger and onions toward the kitchen where my grandmother stood ready to embrace me, because that night, my house smelled just like hers.

How odd to praise the aroma of cabbage and ground beef! In novels written before 1950, the lingering tang of cooked cabbage signals an atmosphere of poverty and despair, while depressing kitchens in modern literature reek of greasy hamburger. But in my German grandmother's warm, clean house, nothing ever smelled rancid or oppressive. Her cooking and baking supplied the indoor world with its own orderly weather: humid clouds from roasting meats and simmering soups, followed by the summery heat of baking bread, pies and cinnamon-scented cookies. These odors gathered like the birds we counted on the telephone wire outside her kitchen window before a storm, only to disappear once the skies cleared.

That October night, nipping at the heels of Halloween, my house was experiencing some of my grandmother's weather. I'd just finished baking my very first batch of the envelopes of yeast dough filled with onions, meat and cabbage her German family brought to Saskatchewan from their settlement on the banks of the Volga. Thirty *berock* were lined up on cooling racks on my kitchen counters, their rounded brown backs still warm to the touch. I'd had my grandmother's recipe ever since my mother forced her to dictate the procedure, converting the measurements from handfuls and pinches to cups and teaspoons, but until recently, I hadn't had the courage to use it. My grandmother had always supplied the family with *berock*, even after she entered her nineties, though by then, she required help from my mother and aunts. For more than two years after her death at the age of a hundred and one, no one in the family, as far as I knew, had tasted one. Perhaps, like me, they had allowed themselves to be satisfied with memories.

This year, my husband and I, bored with the tired charade of Trick or Treat, decided to invite some friends for an All Soul's Day feast. We were encouraging our guests to bring potluck dishes associated with their beloved dead. At first, with my mind on the sugar skulls created for El Dia de Los Muertos, I thought of some of the sweets families use to celebrate life and assuage grief. I remembered the cheesecakes my mother served at her father's birthday every year, my grandmother's full cookie jar and the fussy cakes my friend Patrick used to make from antique cookbooks. Dessert was something I could produce without undue hassle. I'd take the easy way out and make some of my grandmother's famous, often-imitated snicker doodles.

But then I thought of all the family gatherings consecrated by my grandmother's *berock*, how the children were given one to break open on their plates while the grownups took their places at the table. I remember watching little wisps of steam rising from the moist interior before closing my eyes to the murmur of the family prayer. Even with that bit of extra cooling, the first bites were always too hot, as if the thin, evenly browned crust contained a bit of the earth's molten core. Everyone, large and small, ate two or three or four, and even after we'd gorged ourselves, there were always at least a few left over. When I dug the recipe from my files and decided it wasn't beyond my abilities, I finally understood that Gumma wasn't around to make them anymore.

Because I'd never paid attention to the process of sealing the edges of the dough, I called my mother to discuss some of the procedure's finer points. We spoke, then, of my grandmother's inexhaustible energy, her habit of making *berock* in batches of seventy-five or so, which meant seven pounds of flour had to be kneaded and allowed to rise three times while she prepared the filling, cleaned house and set out meals for whoever happened to be visiting. I remembered how, at my request, she and Mom had made more than two hundred *berock* for our wedding reception. It was hardly the kind of entrée a bride might find in a book of perfect wedding meals, but their presence made every guest part of the family. I tried picturing all the cabbages and onions that had to be chopped and sautéed, what neighborhood freezers stored this treasure until the Big Day. Surely I could manage a batch to feed twelve.

I shopped for cabbages and onions with memories of watching my grandmother inspect onions for soft spots, cabbage for heft, potatoes for smooth skins and unsprouted eyes. I knew she'd approve of the sale I found on the hamburger, and while I felt a little guilty buying frozen bread dough instead of the flour and yeast to make it from scratch, I recalled how practical she was. She was known to make noodles by hand, even when she was in her eighties, but she delighted in the few times I set up my noodle maker on her Formica-topped table, and we let the machine do some of the work.

Listening to the clack of the wooden rolling pin as I worked the stretchy bread dough into thin, four-inch squares, I thought of the dinnerware I would use for the party: the blue willow plates like the ones in my other grandparents' spare little kitchen, where the oilcloth-covered table was always set for the next meal and a jar of cocktail onions waited for me in the refrigerator. As soon as I decided to buy some of those little onions for the feast, I thought of the years when my Uncle Phil, a colonel stationed with his family in Germany, would send my brother and me bags of rare gummibarren, a candy never before seen in California. Some gummy bears, then, for Phil, now that they've so thoroughly colonized this territory, and, if I could find them, some marzipan fruits in memory of Bob, a family friend who supplied my first tastes of many things elegant and strange.

With that flood of memories came others, and I spent the long afternoon in my kitchen savoring them. I wondered what was happening in my friends' houses as they prepared for this celebration, which of their departed loved ones they'd bring to the party. As I slid the lumpy pockets of lightly oiled dough into the oven, I knew that my *berock* would never be as good as my grandmother's. She'd been making them for more than fifty years before I ever took my first bite. But when I came inside the house that night to finish cleaning up, I saw how the fragrance had lured my teenaged sons from behind their closed bedroom doors and into the kitchen. I gave each of them one to taste before putting the rest aside for the party, vowing that someday soon, I'd make enough to let them eat all they wanted.

How the Author Makes a Discovery and Shares It in "Feast of All Souls"

In this essay, the comparing and contrasting starts before we even know the essay's topic. Working hard in the kitchen; Susan Bono contrasts the afternoon she saw in full swing to the evening she is surprised to see outside her door. She thinks she ought to smell broccoli steaming, dust and teenaged boys in her kitchen, but instead she smells cabbage and onions and hamburgers. She contrasts herself in her kitchen to her young girl self in her grandmother's kitchen. She compares the aroma of the food she is making to ideas of poverty in the novels she read growing up. She contrasts this idea of poverty with her grandmother's cabbage cooking in a kitchen with its own magical and rich weather over the pots. The odors in her grandmother's kitchen gathered like birds on a telephone wire and disappeared like them. With these comparisons and contrasts, Bono sets up the story she is going to tell: she is preparing for a party on All Soul's Day, and the food she is making brings back memories of a loved one. We will learn about her grandmother's energy in contrast to her own. We will learn about her grandmother's ability to supply loads of *berock* for her granddaughter's wedding, in contrast to the granddaughter's efforts to feed only twelve. The dinner idea contrasts to other ways the author has celebrated Halloween. And the decision to make *berock* contrasts with her earlier plan to make simple snicker doodle cookies. In portraying her grandmother, Bono does decide the two are alike in their trait of practicality. And as a bonus, after coming to terms with the idea that her *berock* will never be as good as her grandmother's, Bono realizes that her cooking has lured her teenage sons from behind their closed doors and into the kitchen. No matter that her *berock* is not as skillfully made as her experienced grandmother's; the cooking has had the same effect on her children as it had on her. In this way, though her *berock* making is not as it should be, it serves her memory and household very well.

Usually, in using comparison and contrast to answer the question, "What in our lives is not as it is supposed to be?" we do find a gem about what it means to be who we are.

Exercises for Developing Your Material

There are two helpful listing exercises you can do to get your mind working along comparison and contrast lines.

Telling It How It Never Was to Find Out How It Is

One of the exercises you can use to help yourself warm up for comparison and contrast thinking is the simile making exercise I introduced in the description chapter. It helps you realize how things that are different are also alike. A doorknob is like a knee. Drop earrings are like tetherballs.

Facility in using constructions like this will help you learn to write comparison and contrast essays. For instance, if you said, "Writing is like mining for gold," you could explain the writing process in terms of gold mining—what equipment is needed, how to pan in the river of information, how to recognize a nugget, and what to do with it. This mining may not be anything like the way you hoped writing would be—well-shaped essays, stories, and poems that appear rapidly on your computer screen, as unstoppable as pedestrians crossing New York's streets.

If you said, "My old boyfriend was like a McDonald's," you might find yourself writing about how unsatisfying the relationship was—the same old menu, the pre-spread ketchup-mustard combo on the rolls meant to please without taking a stand, the flashy packaging over the skimpy meal. This relationship may be nothing like the one you'd hope to have, the one you'd compare to the Louvre filled with beautiful treasures.

To use metaphoric thinking as a warm-up exercise, make a list of people and activities in your life and compare them to things you have never compared them to before. For example: "Arguing is like rowing with one oar" or, "My mother is like a library." Next, take one of the metaphors from your list and extend the analogy, as in the gold panning and writing example or the relationship and

MacDonald's example. Continue talking about one subject in terms of another. Some of what you say may seem silly, but keep going. Metaphorical thinking can help you be brilliant on the page!

In the following example essay, Sam Turner compares writing to playing ball to show us how unrealistic expectations get in the way of our writing.

Writing (Almost Anything) Requires Stepping Up to the Plate.

It's always interesting to me how some people will quit before they start. Whether it is some hidden failure they had in the first grade, or an embarrassing moment sometime in their life, I can tell that they have probably given up before they started: "Oh, I can't sing . . . play the piano . . . dance . . . draw . . . write poetry." You pick the subject; someone will tell you they can't do it. Ask the second question, "Why not?" and the answer is usually, "I never could." Or, "I tried once and . . ."

Yet, these same folks may have been good in baseball, basketball, track, or swimming. They will freely admit that they had to practice in order to become a valuable member of the team. They understand that, no matter how good they are, they are not always going to step to the plate and hit a home run. They might even (perish the thought) actually strike out. They know that they won't stop taking piano lessons just because no one asked them to perform in the symphony after the first lesson. People expect to have to practice the piano, basketball, baseball, or golf. They know it takes months and years of practice.

Why then, are they surprised when they don't hit a "home run" the first time they attempt to draw a picture or write a poem? Place a blank page in front of them and ask them to write something, anything about themselves and they react with panic. I often tell my adult students that, if they can talk, they can write. No one says that the first words they put on the paper will be captured by an agent and sold for a million dollars. Maybe they are afraid of making a mistake. Why do they continue to swing at the ball, shoot for the basket, swing the club? They know that, eventually, things will connect and they'll succeed.

Now, if you are convinced that maybe you can write, just a little, start with something simple. How about a letter to a relative or friend – someone you have been meaning to write to anyway? Tell them that you are planning to take up writing. You could also take a writing workshop or a poetry workshop and let the presenter be your "coach." Join a writer's group. Meet people who enjoy writing. Take a class at your local junior college for non-credit and learn some new techniques for writing. Read books: not just books on writing, but novels, and non-fiction. Read. Gradually, you will begin to prefer the writing styles of some authors better than others. Keep a journal. Write something every day. Even a sentence will do to start. Just think of it as stepping up to the plate.

Before and After

Another exercise I've invented to grease the comparison and contrast mind comes from my interest in "before and after" pictures, from the photos people take of their houses before and after "the remodel" to the ones in magazines showing the results of cosmetic makeovers and diet plans. We are all being remodeled and made over as time goes by.

To do this exercise, make a list of sentences that begin with "before" and continue with "after" such as:

- Before I turned sixteen, I put up with my curly hair; after that I straightened it every month.
- Before my divorce, I lived in a huge old house on a tree-lined street in the artsy part of town; after I remarried I lived in a smaller old house in a working-class part of town.

- Before I was remarried, I never ate pecans on my cereal; after I remarried I looked forward to a whole pile of pecan halves on the Rice Chex in my bowl.
- Before I had children, I didn't know myself; after I had children, I learned more and more about who I am.

Write befores and afters on subjects important and unimportant, physical and spiritual, silly, mundane, and esoteric. Have fun seeking out ways in which you have experienced change. Reread your list. Notice that the changes (contrasts) work against a background of sameness (comparisons). Before and after my divorce, I lived in houses; where and what kind changed. I am still myself before and after having children; the difference is that I know myself better after having children. I ate cereal before and after my remarriage, but what I put on the cereal changed. Don't worry about whether you are comparing and contrasting or whether they are balanced in your writing. Your mind does this kind of thinking naturally.

Locating Your Comparison and Contrast Material

Write the phrase, "It's not the way it's supposed to be" in the center of a blank page. If you are working with a particular topic, think of elements of your experience (our examples have been divorce, parenting, illness, war experience, and visits to foreign countries). How are your experiences in those areas different from what you thought they would be? You might have experienced quiet at the front instead of action, or you might have felt three as a parent instead of thirty-three. You may have felt surprisingly exhilarated during a divorce rather than depressed. Cluster as many of the ways "things are not the way they are supposed to be" on any topic you choose and then get more detailed about the ones that appeal to you to write about.

If you are working without a particular topic, think of circumstances in your life, big and small, that differ from how you'd like them to be or differ from how someone close to you would like them to be. Your cluster may include topics like your job, marriage, home, hobby, vacation, or social behavior. Suppose you are writing about visiting another country; your cluster might include things like how learning the local expressions hindered rather than helped you or how taking the buses turned out to be more fun than using your international driver's license. When you have decided what you want to work on, cluster around the sensory information in the topic—how things tasted, smelled, sounded, felt, and looked. Then begin a freewrite. You might start it out with a "like" construction or a "before and after" sentence. For instance, "When I took my family to the Grand Canyon, I felt like the clown who doesn't see the gun-toting villain coming up behind him. " Or, "When I think about my marriage, I think about those Hi-Q puzzles I had as a kid and the way I seemingly endlessly moved the pegs over one another." Or, "Before I was a part of the group called senior citizens, I thought growing older meant growing wiser." Or, "Before I went to Paris as an exchange teacher, I thought I would spend all my free time there in cafes writing in my journal, but within a few weeks I was farming."

Write for about ten minutes. Whatever your focus, your life is different than you thought it would be or it is different than someone else wishes it were. Keep writing the particulars of each view of your life in this freewrite.

Writing Your Essay

Next, write a draft of a comparison and contrast essay. Begin with an image or anecdote that sets you and your readers in the situation you are writing about. Remember how Susan Bono places herself outside taking trash out after a day of cooking and how Susan Hagen lets us know that she loves softball but wasn't allowed to play because her parents feared her braces would get damaged. You might be inspired by the way novelist Amy Tan began her essay called "Watching Chin," which appeared in the September 1989 issue of *Glamour Magazine*:

> I am an ignorant observer of the situation in China, unversed in politics, a citizen of the United Sates, where "inalienable rights" have been a fact of life from the day I was born.
>
> But over the past few months, I have been watching the televised coverage of events in Beijing . . .

She tells who she is in relation to her subject and what she has taken for granted in her life. Then the word "but" acts a hinge opening the door for contrasting American and Chinese events. In your writing, try beginning with who you are and what you are doing. Then with a "but" enter the domain of how things were supposed to be. Or begin with a description of how things were supposed to be. Then, with a "but," throw yourself into a description of how they actually are.

Once you start, write your draft from beginning to end. Then put it away for a little while and get response before continuing. Do this until you feel that your essay is done. When it is finished, you will have arrived at an important insight about how you feel about your life and written an essay that interests your readers as well.

Chapter VII

The Classification and Division Essay

Write Question #5: What types of people, situations, places, things or events do I experience in my life?

> *And where did I find, other than in living day to day, the sense of the complex that made such sense to me?*
>
> —Marvin Bell
> *Writers on Writing*
> edited by Robert Pack and Jay Parnini

Sometimes comedian and speakers entertain audiences by proclaiming something like: "There are three kinds of people—those who do such-and-such, those who do this-and-that, and those who do neither. " They usually draw examples and provide names for each type.

In the course of life, you, too, recognize types of people and their behavior, as well as types of places, situations, things, and events. When you organize your writing according to categories, you can inform and entertain others.

In a classification and division essay, you divide your subject into groups according to a distinguishing trait each group has in common. It is important to have at least three groups; otherwise you are in the realm of comparison and contrast. Your skills with description and narration, how-to, and comparison and contrast will help you write to evoke and explain the categories and their differences as well as move your essay along.

In a column that appeared in *The New York Times* in 1968 and is reprinted in *The Riverside Reader,* Volume II, edited by Joseph Timmer and Maxine Hairston, author Russell Baker takes on the voice of a professor to explain the three major categories of inanimate objects: "those that don't work, those that break down and those that get lost." The categories are introduced according to the intensity with which they vex humankind. I laugh when I read this essay because I get in touch with my usually unconscious, though unavoidable, frustration with the objects in my life.

Be original when you ask yourself, "What types of people, situations, places, things, or events do I experience in my life?" Your list might include types of waiters and waitresses, types of responses you get from machines, types of cell phone users, types of Sundays, and types of neighbors. Make your list original by narrowing down categories that occur to you. For instance, if you write down supermarket shoppers, try dividing the category into types by characteristics: types of cart pushers or the ways people accept food samples at demonstration tables.

If you have a topic you already want to explore, insert that topic into the "write" question. For instance, using the examples from before, if you are writing about parenting you might say, "What situations in parenting do I know enough about to illustrate by using categories?" If you are writing about visiting a new country, do the same thing: "What situations from visiting this new country can I evoke by using categories?" In the case of parenting, you might think of kinds of childhood misbehaviors, kinds of school conferences, kinds of requests children make of parents, and kinds of requests parents make of children, among other categories. About visiting a new country, your categories might turn out to be types of responses you get when you tell people you have done that, types of medical problems to prepare for, types of sadness you experienced away from home, types of locals you met there, types of tourists you met, or types of tours.

Before you work on gathering the answers to your "write" question, turn your attention to the example essays and discussions that follow.

Example Division and Classification Essays

In the following essay by Susan Luzader, readers look through the eyes of a parent confronted with her son's driving mishaps. As you read the essay, notice Luzader's introduction to her material and then the way she designates each mishap by the particular way her son Justin avoids calling it a real car accident. Notice the details she uses to describe each accident, the narrative approach she uses to tell how it happened, and the way she orders the accidents. Although they have characteristics in common, each successive mishap has new distinguishing characteristics as well.

The Accidental Student

Until I had a teenage son, I never realized ripping the bumper off a car is not a real accident. I always considered any damage to a vehicle as an accident, but my son has spent much of the past three years teaching me otherwise. There are accidents that are not really accidents, accidents that don't count because the judge concedes it wasn't your fault, and then there are accidents involving more than cars.

I got my first lesson about three months after Justin acquired his driver's license. One autumn afternoon he poked his head into the kitchen to inform me he was taking his little brother to Walgreen's for shampoo and other essentials and would be back in less than a half an hour. He was overly optimistic. As I chopped red and yellow peppers for fajitas, I heard the men painting the outside of my house laughing. I smiled, enjoying their mirth, and resumed chopping.

Sweeping the strips into my hands, turning to place them into a bowl, I realized Justin and his brother were standing in the kitchen doorway, watching me work. I rinsed my hands and asked if they needed something. The silence alerted me. Justin shuffled his feet, cleared his throat, and said I needed to go out and look at his car. Why? I asked. "You just need to, Mom."

Stepping out the front door, I noticed the two painters nudging themselves as they sat on the courtyard wall. Justin's car, an 11-year-old BMW his grandparents had sold to him, was at the end of the driveway, its bumper lying on the ground, intact. He'd hooked it on the cement post at the end of the driveway, popping it off. When we took it to the welding shop to be reattached, the welder told Justin he should hire my son because he'd never seen a bumper taken off so cleanly. Justin's chest puffed with pride.

Justin refused to consider this an accident because he'd paid to have the bumper put back on and it was never reported to the insurance company. No matter what I said, he maintained his driving record was clean.

The next summer, Justin was working two jobs, one as a delivery driver for a sandwich shop and one for his dad to pay for car insurance. One morning he asked if he could borrow my car because his air conditioning wasn't working and I agreed. I got a phone call from Justin around 1:30, saying I had to come to the sandwich shop, that something had happened. After impatient questioning, it was revealed that "something" was damage to my car. Luckily, it was a station wagon so the bumper fit comfortably in the back. Once more, the welder offered my son a job.

When school started that fall, Justin helped earn gas money by driving four seventh-graders to school. I got the phone call every mom dreads about 7:45 one crisp fall morning—Justin and several others had tangled their cars on Sunrise. Hyperventilating and muttering prayers, I sped to the accident scene to find the seventh graders eager to miss the Latin test and flicking gravel at each other. "It wasn't my fault," Justin greeted me, although I had my doubts. Luckily for him, the judge agreed and once more, Justin declared his driving record clean.

For graduating high school, Justin's dad gave him a pickup truck and many stern warnings about his driving behavior and accepting responsibility. Justin reminded us he'd never really caused an accident and drove off to college. We'd bought the truck because it was safe, a shelter for our reckless son, but big trucks can cause big damage, especially when the driver is distracted by four girls riding with him in the cab.

It was a simple accident, the truck and a BMW 750 both refusing to give way as two lanes narrowed to one in the winding streets of La Jolla. The truck was undamaged, doing the job we assigned it, but the Beemer had a crease along both doors, and a driver with a temper who jumped out of her car, pounding on Justin's window, demanding justice. "It will be fine," my husband told a shaken Justin over the phone, "the insurance company will find you both 50 percent liable, and you can pay the deductible."

A few days later, the police faxed a copy of the accident report to our insurance agent, who informed my husband that Justin admitted the accident was his fault. "I guess I just wasn't paying attention," he told the officer. The woman is claiming $4,000 in medical bills and wants two new doors and a new driver's seat.

"Now, now he accepts responsibility," my husband moaned, breaking out in shingles three days later.

Justin's insurance rates will most likely go up now, no matter how much he rants about how the woman is cheating the insurance company. The company knows, but will throw her a few thousand dollars to go away. "It was an accident; I didn't mean to say that," he tells us. He has learned the hard way that accidents of the mouth can often cause more damage than those involving vehicles.

How the Writer Makes a Discovery and Shares It
in "The Accidental Student"

Written after an accident that Luzader believes was not Justin's fault alone, this essay is a humorous look at a teenager's passage from denying responsibility to accepting responsibility and learning society's sometimes odd response.

Luzader builds to a climax in her essay by looking at the characteristics of each accident: where she was and what she was doing when she found out about the accident, what happened, what others said, what her son said, and what the family did to fix and replace vehicles. At the essay's climax, the son who couldn't call what he had an accident, suddenly accidentally says something that proves costly to the family. The family had worked toward instilling responsible driving behavior in the son, whose accident vocabulary differed from their own. Ultimately, Justin used their vocabulary, only to learn that it is best to be as careful about terminology outside his home as in it.

In the following classification and division essay, Joanne Rocklin classifies children's book writers. She represents the divisions she sees by describing the temperaments of her writing cats Samtoo, Manny, and Moe. According to Rocklin, each cat has a distinct sensibility that lends itself to meeting the demands of writing a particular kind of children's book.

Why Cats Write

I recently discovered that my three cats write children's books. They decided they would no longer listen to my work unless I listened to theirs. I agreed. I enjoy their scribblings, and often spend my time listening to them read when I should be working at the computer. In any case, I would like to discuss the topic, "Finding One's Voice" and "Choosing a Genre When Writing for Children," using my cats' endeavors as examples.

It is interesting how reading background, temperament and talent are all involved in deciding what sort of children's book to write. My fifteen-year-old tabby, Samtoo, writes picture books and poetry. Samtoo revels in the loveliness of the small detail, for example the sparkle of a horse fly's bug-eye or the melodious "pop" of a can of Fancy Feast. She is a dainty feline who appreciates routine and security, thus enjoying the patterns of rhyme and rhythm. However, she does find a clever surprise at the end of a poem or picture book as intoxicating as catnip!

Samtoo knows that a picture book is almost always thirty-two pages long. Her current challenge is honing down her latest manuscript, *Millions of Fleas*. Samtoo's pet peeve is the careless use of metaphor and simile, reminding me the other day that "quiet as a mouse" certainly does not apply to any mouse she's torn apart and eaten!

Manny, a black and white, meticulously groomed short-hair, prefers writing juvenile nonfiction. He is a practical cat who enjoys research, and has expanded many a hobby or scholarly interest into a fascinating nonfiction project. Manny knows that only those cats who can write clearly and succinctly should attempt this genre. Children like their nonfiction understandable and up-to-date. They also enjoy a new twist to a topic. For example, Manny's current interests are chicken and hairballs. Understanding that books about chicken are everywhere this year, he is still pondering what he can add to the field. But hairballs! No mention in *Books in Print*! So far the working title of this project is "Great Hairballs of the Twentieth Century." I told him I thought he'd bit off more than he could swallow. On the other hand, perhaps I'm envious of his obvious excitement as he prepares his query letter to editors. Excited writers make for excited readers, Manny knows!

Moe is a scruffy, long-haired gray cat with tuna breath. He's seen a lot of the underside of life—under cars, cellars, beds— you name it. Moe fancies himself a private eye, skulking along walls, leaping out suddenly from behind doors. Mysterious noise? Moe will investigate. Intriguing, exotic smell? There is Moe again. Moe is everywhere and nowhere, taking it all in. Been around and played around and lived to tell about it. And tell about it he does! In sharp, tense prose Moe writes terrific adventure-mystery novels for youngsters. Moe is NOT nice when he creates his stories. Nice is not where it's at, he growls. To capture even the most reluctant young reader, to get that reader turning pages, you gotta be spittin' mean. You gotta create tension and conflict to get your story rolling. Then you tie it all up in the end, tight and neat as a new ball of string. Hey, it works for Moe, who just sold the paperback rights to his popular Sam Spayed series for youngsters.

So why do Samtoo, Manny and Moe write? Why do I write, for that matter? None of us is famous; we hardly earn enough to live on, not even Moe. And why do we write for children? Are we writing for the child (or kitty) we once were, attempting to constantly recreate the delicious discovery of reading and books?

I've actually posed these questions to my cats. The three of them stared at me disdainfully, then gave the obvious answer.

Meow.

How the Writer Makes a Discovery and Shares It in "Why Cats Right"

By telling us about the temperament and interests that make it possible to write particular kinds of children's books (picture books, juvenile nonfiction and fiction), Joanne Rocklin explains why she writes children's books. She writes because she has the personality to write. Those aspects of her personality that she recognizes in her cats make writing a natural act for her, as natural as her cats' meows. She orders her introductions of the cats and the kind of books each writes according to the characteristic that distinguishes the level of the children's book: first picture books, then books about the characteristics of things in the world, and then stories with adventure and complication. By the time we have considered the cats and their personalities and how they put those personalities into their books, we have received genuine knowledge about writing for children. We leave the essay informed about what it takes (a sense of delight in life above all!) to write for children.

A Word on Logical Subdivisions

When you write division and classification essays to explore and inform, remember to provide at least three content divisions. This helps you appear authoritative. When you offer only two subdivisions—"this way" or "not this way"—readers may be tempted to think of more categories and not trust your perception. In addition, your writing may compare and contrast rather than divide and classify. Logical division requires that there be a single governing principle to the divisions—phone calls from my mother, responses I have to my "ex," kinds of English teachers, kinds of fathers—and that the divisions seem comprehensive.

Dividing stores into kinds like department stores, convenience stores, and boutiques is not comprehensive. These categories leave out many kinds of stores—shoe stores, country general stores, electronic and appliances stores, furniture stores, and warehouse shopping stores, among others. There is no way you could cover all the kinds of stores when they are divided this way without writing a telephone book. When categories are this large, you must think of a new principle upon which to base your subdivisions. Find a principle that allows you to deal with a certain chunk of the broader classification and provides a framework for looking at your subject. For example, if you worded your category, "the three kinds of stores I shop in," the subdivisions department stores, convenience stores, and boutiques would seem odd but comprehensive.

Dividing stores into groups such as stores tourists like, stores community members like, and second-hand stores disrupts having a consistent principle of organization—the last kind of store could belong to either category or both. A division such as stores I like, stores my husband likes, and stores my children like is consistent and complete for purposes of organization. So are divisions like stores in my city that tourists like, stores in my city that residents like, and stores in my city that residents of neighboring communities like. So are divisions like stores I use daily, stores I use monthly, and stores I use once a year.

Exercises for Developing Your Material

A New, Whirled Order

Here is an exercise for thinking along division and classification lines. Brainstorm a page-long list of things, people, places, events and situations you don't usually think of in categories but ones you feel you could: freeway drivers, bosses, billboard ads, radio programs, food in your pantry, people ordering coffee, people walking their dogs, mothers, fathers, daughters, sons, workers, people courting, phone-machine message styles. After you have brainstormed a page of areas to categorize, take a few of the ideas and create some subdivisions for them. I might divide food in my pantry into groups by thinking of food as viewed through the eyes of a teenage boy: pop-it-into-your-mouth-whenever-you-are-hungry food, consider-if-you-can-pop-it-into-your-mouth-even-though-it-would-taste-better-cooked food, and overlook-it-all-together-because-it-takes-more-than-10-minutes-to-prepare food.

You might enjoy sitting down with a group and having everyone write down on separate pieces of paper various kinds of things, people, situations, and events: parental lectures, punishments, downtowners, ways to spend quality time, collectors, music buffs. Have everyone fold up their pieces of paper and drop them into a bowl or a hat. Everyone then selects the same number of pieces from the hat as they put into it. Next, they think of original ways to subdivide the classifications they selected. Listening to everyone's categories and ideas about subdividing them loosens up everyone's thinking and bolsters the search for original ways to make divisions and subdivisions based on life experience.

The principle you use to subdivide your subject should be one that communicates an original outlook, a new way of viewing the classification of everyday things. Ultimately this principle provides a way of viewing your own behaviors as well as that of others.

Locating Your Division and Classification Material

Perhaps while practicing dividing and clarifying, you found a topic you would like to write about or perhaps you are using a topic you've been interested in for a while. To use our examples again, ask, "What things, people, places, situations, and events in my divorce, my parenting, my illness, my war experience, or my visit to a foreign country do I know enough about to illustrate by subdividing into categories?" Concerning divorce, for instance, you might think of such categories as responses of friends to your singlehood, inept ways people try to take care of you, and cold shoulders encountered since you have not been part of a couple. Whether you have a topic you've been using for all of your essays or a new one for this style essay, put the words "things, people, places, and events I can divide" in the center of a page to start a cluster. If you want, do a separate cluster for each of the four words. After you cluster from these words, you will find a topic that interests you. Put that topic in the middle of a blank page and do a cluster around it. Shoot off all the subtypes you can think of from the central word, circle them, and then off of those circles, cluster traits and examples of each type. Allow yourself to be silly and farfetched. You never know where one image will lead or when a silly idea will uncover a brilliant one. What do your subdivisions have in common? Are they about what bugs you, what amuses you, what makes you angry, what you think is most important to know? Have you been able to subdivide your selected category into at least three divisions? On what basis have you made the subdivisions? The answers to these three questions will help you start a freewrite.

Do a ten-minute freewrite on a topic that interests you from your clusters. When you are ready, write a first draft of your classification and division essay. You can start with a short anecdote in which you re-experience why this discussion is important in your life. For instance, if I were going to write about my behaviors as a writer, I might start with a scene relating the last time I grumbled at my family saying I was going to give up writing, buy a suit, and look for a job downtown. This would lead me into writing about my writing behaviors, which I could categorize as ignoring writing, accusing my family of taking up all my time, having outbursts and locking myself up with my computer. As unlike writing as some of these behaviors appear, they are for me all part of a cycle toward getting down to writing.

Another way to begin a division and classification essay is by announcing your categories and why you are presenting them. Look again at how Susan Luzader starts her essay about her son's accidents. The opening paragraph announces whom she is learning from and what she is learning: "Until I had a teenage son, I never realized ripping the bumper off a car is not a real accident . . . my son has spent much of the past three years teaching me otherwise." Then she tells us what she's learned by classifying and dividing: "There are accidents that are not really accidents, accidents that don't count because the judge concedes it wasn't your fault, and then there are accidents involving more than cars." We're set to read and find out about these sub-divisions from her son's perspective.

Joanne Rocklin also starts her essay with a statement. Having recently learned that her cats write for children, she decides to discuss the "big" topics of "Finding One's Voice" and "Choosing a Genre When Writing for Children" and to focus on her cats' endeavors as examples. Because she addresses her topic in a fresh way, those who have already read extensively on writing for children will pay attention and those who are new to the topic will enjoy receiving concrete information about what is so often theoretical.

Whether you start your essay with an anecdote or an announcement, write your draft from beginning to end. The divisions you make will take over and direct your thoughts. In addition, the essay styles you are already familiar with will come to aid you as you write: Description helps you evoke subdivisions with precise images. Narration helps with little stories inside the divisions, both to further evoke them and to let your readers know why you chose to explore a particular subject. Comparison and contrast helps you make transitions from one subdivision to the next and distinguish the differences among the divisions. How-to can even make its way into a division and classification essay if you instruct your readers on how to classify something they might not have thought of classifying!

As you rely on sensory images and particulars, you will instinctively use all these organizational styles to make connections and travel toward discovery.

Developing the Draft

When you read your first draft to others, it may seem incompletely formed and even annoying if it leaves them without understanding your logic in making the categories. Use any annoyance you hear as encouragement to develop your writing. Note the responses you get to the divisions you make and to your overall category. Note the responses to how you introduce your topic, order it, and move from one division to another, and finally to how you exit your essay. Pay attention to the descriptions that delight others and those that confuse or bother them. Use this information to pinpoint opportunities for a successful revision.

Chapter VIII

The Cause and Effect Essay

Write Question #6: What decisions or actions have I or someone else made or taken that have affected my life and what are those effects?

> *If we are able to make the best sense of our lives—if we persist in trying to do so and truly commit ourselves to this task—perhaps we can even affect the course of history and change the flow of events. Who knows?*
> —Malcolm Boyd
> *Edges, Boundaries, and Connections*

You are familiar with reading the cause and effect style in newspapers and books. You may have read articles that report on FAA investigations of plane crashes. To answer the question what made a plane crash, the FAA investigates material, equipment, weather, and human causes. A thorough investigation may show which sequence of events and problems caused the crash.

You may have read books in which historians and social scientists study the causes of Nazism and the rise of Hitler, the rise and fall of communism, or the reasons behind economic failures. Medical researchers write articles exploring causes of diseases. They want to know why there is a sudden upswing in the number of tuberculosis or meningitis cases reported.

When something happens to you, you may ask, "Why did this happen to me?" "Why did I do what I did?" This is a natural way to think. However, in our culture, we are so used to using hindsight to find causes in the hopes of applying knowledge to future situations, we forget the wisdom of looking further down the chain to examine the effects of decisions and actions. Sometimes there is no discernable "why" for a situation. It is just there. It is important to discover "what " has happened in you as a result of that situation.

"What decisions or actions have I or someone else made or taken that have affected my life and what are those effects?" You may find yourself remembering your parents' decision to move, have another child, or send you to camp. You might remember your decision to enter college a decade after high school graduation. You might think of your decision to seek or not to seek a promotion at work. You might think of a best friend's decision to move across the country. You might think of a time you were a victim of a burglary or con artist.

The question can be adapted to your area of writing interest by inserting your topic: What decisions or actions have I or someone else made or taken concerning (to use our usual examples once again) my parenting, divorcing, illness, fighting, or visiting, and what are the effects of those decisions on my life? Perhaps you moved to a retirement community, or became a single parent, or left Morocco before you wanted to, or suddenly enlisted in the army.

Using the cause and effect style is valuable in personal essays written for self-discovery. Many of us believe that we cannot change our circumstances, mood, or behavior because such and such a thing happened to us. However, as writers when we apply cause-and-effect thinking to personal essay writing, our behavior, circumstances, and moods do begin to change. To write this kind of essay, we don't have to limit our thinking to the one or two most pivotal times in our lives. In 1909, Mark Twain wrote an essay called "The Turning Point in My Life," which appeared in *Harper's Bazaar*. In it he said, "I know we have a fashion of saying 'such and such an event was the turning-point in my life,' but we shouldn't say it. We should merely grant that its place as last link in the chain makes it the most conspicuous link . . ." It is Life with a big L that hands us the causes; the effects of those causes create the weave of our lives.

To write cause and effect personal essays that help you reach discovery and new ways of seeing, think in specifics. Write down details about the decisions and actions that affected you and the consequences of these decisions and actions—the frown on your mother's face, the way her checked apron was blowing in the wind, the drawer you keep that apron in today. Your story and experience will emerge from these details. Moreover, when choosing the decision or action you will write about, remember that making it about something specific helps. It may prove more rewarding to center an essay on not going to a dance on your night off as a camp counselor and consequently meeting the man who was to become your husband than to write about how meeting your husband changed your life.

Example Description Essays

In the following sample essays, you will experience the effects on one writer of living in New York City during the September 11, 2001 World Trade Center tragedy and the effects on another writer of his father's discovery that his son wanted to be a poet. As you read the two sample essays in this chapter, watch for the way the writers introduce the incident that is the "cause" part of the essay and the way they introduce and handle the "effects." Notice especially the way the writers use description, narration, and comparison and contrast patterns in telling their cause and effect story.

Janice Eidus announces that for four years she has been unable to keep the idea of having a child out of her mind, but she has also been unable to decide to raise a child. She compares the baby lust with the actuality of having a child. It is when history intervenes that she is propelled forward in her decision-making.

Baby Lust

For the past few years, John and I have been agonizing over whether or not to have a child. Our lives are full. For most of our marriage, we've been happy with our decision to be childfree. We've been oblivious to the charms of squalling infants and overly precocious toddlers; we've vastly preferred our cats. So why, about four years ago, did I begin yearning for a child?

I don't know. But I do know that I've tried very hard to talk myself out of these yearnings. They're "trite," I tell myself, and "foolishly romantic." After all, my friends with children are no happier than I; some of them are far less happy, feeling trapped in loveless marriages. One friend, who has two small girls, widowed young, is chronically in mourning. Another, once an up-and-coming visual artist, has put his career on hold for almost 15 years, working as a businessman to put his two boys through private schools. Another has a son who's a heroin addict.

But my yearnings won't go away: I spend many sessions discussing them with my therapist. She (a mother and grandmother herself) doesn't want to "discourage" me, but she wants me "to be realistic." "You'll have far less time to write than you do now," she says, "and you already complain about not having enough time. And you'll be utterly exhausted." Relentless, she continues "It will probably be difficult for you to get pregnant. You may have to adopt." "And," she says, at last truly frightening me, "nothing puts more strain on a marriage than having children. Your relationship with John will radically change."

So we agree to put the idea of having a child to bed.

But the reality is this: I still feel "baby lust" whenever I pass a mother or nanny out with a little one. If the baby is laughing and cooing, my envy level reaches stratospheric heights. When a baby cries anywhere in my vicinity—on the bus or subway, at a nearby table in a coffee shop—I have to stifle the urge to rise and gather her up in my arms.

And then on the morning of 9-11-01, at a little after nine o'clock, I find myself standing out on Sixth Avenue in the West Village, a few blocks from my apartment, just a couple of miles from the World Trade Center, close enough to feel that I can reach out and touch the flames. I watch as the second plane hits, watch as the buildings burn and disintegrate, crumbling like cigarettes.

From 10:30 that morning, and for the next few weeks, John and his colleagues at St. Vincent's work 24-7 administering desperately needed crisis assistance to all those who descend upon the hospital (soon to be known as the "Ground Zero hospital"): the 6,000 family members and friends seeking news of their loved ones; the shell-shocked lucky ones who somehow managed to escape; firefighters and police. (And even now as I write these words four months later, he and his staff are still working overtime helping those in need: small schoolchildren who witnessed bodies falling from the sky; families now in deep mourning; residents displaced from their homes; and so many more of the psychologically wounded).

So I spend the rest of 9-11 (and the next few days) with my friend Jaime who lives a few blocks away from me. For hours, he and I sit side by side in my living room, grasping each other's hands as we watch CNN with disbelief. Then we head outside to buy supplies, food, and clothing from the few stores in our neighborhood that are open. We walk a few blocks west to the temporary morgue that's been set up, where donations are being accepted for workers at Ground Zero.

And throughout all this, even as I stand on line at the morgue, even as I experience a kind of sorrow I never could have imagined I would feel in my lifetime, I can't stop envisioning myself with a child—with my child— by my side, my child whom I will nurture, comfort, mentor, love and protect, who will inspire me to work harder to make the world a safer and better place, a world in which such a terrible thing won't happen again.

I hand over the coffee and bagels, heavy socks, flashlights, and batteries that Jaime and I have brought to the morgue, and I promise myself that when things have settled down a bit, when John and I can open our apartment windows without breathing in thick, overwhelmingly putrid smoke, when the National Guard ceases patrolling our block, when he and I can walk freely in our neighborhood without having to show I.D., when he at last has a free evening in which to begin to relax and unwind, I will tell him as gently as possible that the subject of our becoming parents hasn't been put to bed, after all. And I feel hopeful—confident, actually—as I begin to retrace my steps home from the morgue—that now he will feel the same way.

How the Writer Makes a Discovery and Shares It in "Baby Lust"

What drives the author of this essay beyond the struggle to make a decision is the fact that amidst grave loss, the urge to nurture life is unstoppable. The essay starts by filling the reader in on the life decision Eidus and her husband had seemingly put behind them preceding the events in New York on Sept. 11, 2001. As she describes the rescue efforts and her personal actions (effects told as narration) of providing help, Eidus reveals her inner thoughts (more effects) and how she intends to approach her husband (additional effects) and hopes that the decision to have a child is still alive in him. By describing outer events as well as inner events, she hooks together the day's news and demands with her life's ongoing personal agenda. Janice Eidus reveals that wanting a child remains pervasive for her even though her desire seems contrary to what she thinks she wants (comparison and contrast). Her desire to nurture a child might also be the most sane and loving response she can have to great tragedy.

In "A Close Call," James Bertolino uses the cause and effect style to record an astonishing close call in his life. As a high school student, he wrote poetry and his father's thinking about poetry and poets almost caused young Bertolino to take desperate action.

A Close Call

It happened during the summer between my junior and senior years in high school. I wrote poetry—not just love poems to girl-friends, or somber expressions of alienation and pain, but poems about experiences and ideas. I'd read about the Beat Generation in *Time* magazine, amazed to learn that Wordsworth was not the last poet the world had seen. My older sister—always the co-conspirator—brought home books for me from the local college library: titles by Jack Kerouac, Gregory Corso and, most important, Allen Ginsberg, whose long poem "Howl" wrenched me away from my embrace of pretty verse.

In the spring, after having written a clutch of poems wild with the abrasions of reality, and in a Midwestern version of the voice of Ginsberg, I sent them off to Vantage Press. As many aspiring poets have learned, Vantage is a fairly respectable vanity press that advertises widely their passionate desire to publish your poetry—of course, their intention is to do so with your money. Managing to steer clear of privately funded vanity publication was not, however, the close call I'm writing of here.

My father and I shared the same name, and when the professional-looking manila envelope arrived in July, apparently addressed to him, he opened it without a second thought—that is, until he found the poetry inside. Despite the encouraging words employed by the Vantage editors—the "creative imagination" in my use of language and imagery, and the "promising talent"—my father found the poems horrifying. They were clear evidence of what he'd begun to suspect—his first son, and namesake, was insane.

My mother was the one who told me my poetry manuscript had been intercepted, and that he'd been making phone calls investigating the possibility of some psychiatric counseling for his demented offspring. When after a few days I finally received my parcel, and read the words that validated my secret passion for poetry, I was wounded and confused: how could my father think my lines were proof of madness instead of genius? But the ultimate blow was yet to be delivered.

Again it was my mother who informed me that, after learning the cost of psychiatric counseling, my father concluded what I really needed was the attention of a priest. He arranged for me to visit our man-of-the-cloth on Sunday afternoon. I was deranged with depression and fury.

On Saturday evening, after walking blindly for what seemed like hours, I found myself at a building site for new college classrooms. Above me the dark, overcast sky was a metaphor for my emotions. I began to climb the 75-foot high construction crane, determined to take my life. At the top, carefully avoiding the greasy pulley as I clung, swaying, over the dry, packed dirt far below, I indulged myself in a vision of my own funeral. The casket was closed, surrounded by flowers. Linda, the only girl I'd ever really loved, and lost, was there, head bowed, body wracked with loud sobbing. Off to the side I saw my mother, being supported by my sisters, and behind her, slowly nodding his head, was my father. He was talking to one of my uncles. I could hear him saying, "Yeah . . . I expected something like this. He was crazy, you know. He was loony. But we loved him just the same."

I was so stunned I almost fell off the crane! My suicide would prove him right. So I climbed down, more determined with each shaky rung—I would be a poet, and someday my father (who loved me) would be proud.

*How the Writer Makes a Discovery and Shares It
in "A Close Call"*

Sandwiched between an opening that sets the time of the essay "during the summer between my junior and senior years in high school," and a closing that opens time up with the word "someday," Bertolino writes about the time he made and reversed a suicide decision because he couldn't stand the idea of his father accepting his son's death as the logical consequence of poetry. To prove his father wrong about poets, Bertolino had to abandon thoughts of taking his own life. He would have to stay alive, write poems he believed in, and think that someday, his father would understand his genius and be proud. Reading Bertolino's account, I wonder if all coming of age tales use cause and effect.

Exercises for Developing Your Material

One Thing Leads to Another

Two or more friends or family members can help you get warmed up for cause and effect thinking. Get together and have everyone write three bogus "facts," on separate pieces of paper. Here are three examples: four out of every five dogs are barking more loudly this year than last year; all restaurant workers in the state of Washington now wear green clothes both at work and outside of work; the normal wintertime temperature in Seattle is 82 degrees with low humidity.

After writing down the "facts," each person passes their three papers to others in the group. On the papers received, everyone writes something that could result from the "fact" they see at the top. For instance: Now that dogs bark more loudly, there are fewer house break-ins, but tensions between neighbors are worse because no one is sleeping very well. Since restaurant workers began wearing green clothes all the time, workers in other fields have adopted particular colors for their clothes, and now at parties, no one ever asks the question, "What do you do?" With higher winter temperatures, Seattle has become a vacation paradise, and people there are turning their homes into bed and breakfast places. In addition to community gardens called pea patches, there are now community swimming pools called plunge patches.

When everyone is finished writing down effects for the "facts," pass the lists once again. This time, each person looks at the "facts" as well as the effects written on the pages in front of them. Everyone thinks of some reasons (causes) for these "facts." In my examples, dog food companies began injecting dog food with a certain hormone to increase shelf life, and it affected the dogs' barks. There was a severe hepatitis outbreak in Washington State, and having restaurant workers wear green made it possible to manage the epidemic. Global warming gave Seattle a tropical climate. Listen to what your group has thought up.

If you can't do this exercise with others, skim some newspapers or magazine ads. Write down some of the claims manufacturers make for their products, putting each claim on a separate piece of paper. Chose a few of the claims and write your own ideas of what the results of such a "truth" might be. Next write reasons for the validity of the claims. Let your imagine go.

For instance, I open a magazine and see an ad for a CD. "This recording will replace what you used to expect from music," the ad proclaims. Writing the effects of this claim, I state: "I now expect to hear vacuum cleaner noise when I put my stereo on. I expect not to have to eat anymore once I play the CD I bought. I expect to meet the recording artist in a virtual reality software package that comes along with the CD." Then, when I write the causes for this claim, I think: "The producers wanted to transform the sound of background music. The producers wanted to make a lot of money. The producers wanted to pass off what they had recorded already without spending more money on a better recording."

Inventing results before thinking about causes and inventing causes without thinking about results loosens up your thinking so you can absorb the fact that although one thing leads to another, we can still be surprised at the results. In our society, we rely on cause and effect for analysis in order to control, in order to preserve the idea that we are in charge and can conquer and shape our environment and lives or at least learn how to. However, in writing from personal experience using the cause and effect style, we can cultivate a different kind of understanding and a desire to increase our perception beyond what we might ordinarily conclude.

Locating Your Cause and Effect Material

Viewing circumstances as having been touched off by a decision helps you examine some of the things that have happened in your life. To do this, ask the "write" question: "What decision have I or someone else made that affected my life?" Begin a cluster with the words "decision" in the middle of the blank page. Cluster all the decisions you can think of that you made or that were made for you or that others made for themselves that had effects on you. Cluster images and phrases around each of the decisions that occur to you. Next ask yourself, "What action have I or someone else taken that has affected my life?" Start a cluster with the word "action" in the middle of the page.

If you are exploring a particular topic, insert it into the question like this before you do your clusters: What decision concerning _____ did I or someone else make that has affected me? What action concerning this have I or someone else taken and how has that affected me?

Between these two questions, much will come to mind. Did you decide to marry someone or not to? Did you spend your money seemingly foolishly and enjoy something wonderful, contrary to what others predicted? Did you go through this doorway instead of that one? Did you grow because you surrendered something hard to let go? Did you refuse to surrender in the face of everything and receive something important?

When you feel interested in a particular memory, whether it is on your previously chosen topic or a new one, start a freewrite. Do a "This Is A Poem" exercise if you need to come up with more details about the decision or action you are writing about and its effects on you.

Writing the Essay

Now that you have gathered details through these exercises, select one of the decisions or actions that interests you and begin writing a draft that shows and explores the effects it had on you. Look back at the example essays. Notice how they both start with a mention of time—the last four years for Janice Eidus and the summer between two high school years for James Bertolino. Perhaps you will start your draft by telling when something that turned out to be of consequence happened or by telling what you were thinking about when it happened.

Writer Michael Dorris begins a cause and effect section of "Fetal Alcohol Syndrome, A Parent's Perspective," written for the Centers for Disease Control and now collected in his 1994 book, *Paper Trail,* by getting right to the point: "When you're a parent of an FAS or FAE child, your goals change with the passing years." He then goes on to examine the effects of adopting a fetal alcohol syndrome child on his own sense of self and value as a parent.

You might start with the cause, or you might start with dialog, one in which someone is speaking to you about the decision or one in which you are talking to yourself or others about the decision. The dialog you use may be one you overheard about events that would change your life.

Whatever you do to start writing, include images of where you are, bits of dialog from the time you are remembering, and statements about the cause itself. Try to write from beginning to end. Trust your dexterity in using sensory detail, events organized through time, contrasts, comparisons, how-tos, and divisions and classifications (Janice Eidus divides the reasons why she shouldn't want a child into categories and James Bertolino classifies kinds of poetry he is paying attention to). If those styles can help you, they will occur to you as you are writing, arriving as needed.

Developing the Draft

When you write in the cause and effect style, you must not judge yourself too harshly. Even if it doesn't seem so at first, whatever you choose to write about will ultimately put you in the good light of being honest and capable of self-reflection. Reading drafts to those you trust will provide the responses you need—the Velcro words, feelings, and curiosity—to keep writing and fully tell your story.

Remember, you are discovering the ways in which you are different today as a consequence of the decision or life circumstance you are writing about. If you are not satisfied with your second draft, get new response and redraft until you feel you and your readers understand the ways you changed because of a life situation.

Chapter IX

The Definition Essay

Write Question #7: What role do I play in life that I can name and describe?

> *By itself, nothing "out there" has any definition without a perceiver.*
> —Deepak Chopra, M.D.
> *Unconditional Life: Discovering the Power to Fulfill Your Dreams*

*H*earing-impaired, diabetic, daughter, mother, wife, husband, father, son, teacher, student, refugee, head of household, adoptee, caregiver for an Alzheimer's patient, construction worker, office temp, the "good" one, the black sheep, "them." If some of those words describe you, you are in a position to more fully understand their meaning using the definition essay. Writing this fuller meaning is what essayists call an "extended" definition.

In a definition essay, a writer explores a subject by describing the qualities that distinguish it from any other subject. Division and classification is inherent in definition, because to define something we must identify what classification it belongs to and how it is alike or different (comparison and contrast) from other divisions. Writers often define a subject by listing what qualities it does not have. This is a way of showing the boundaries, the uniqueness of the subject under discussion. Writers usually offer examples to clarify their definitions. Sometimes, these are in the form of anecdotes or short narrations, and they always include description. Ultimately, even how-to and cause and effect become parts of an extended definition essay. How something functions, for instance, can be part of defining it. The cause and effect style helps a writer with definition when the writer explores the results of having or being something.

Here are some more examples of how the cause and effect and how-to styles of essay writing help in writing a personal extended definition essay: A definition of "bus driver" can come from showing how one learns to be a bus driver. Defining what it means to be a daughter can include the effect a daughter's behavior has on her parents. Defining what it means to be a mother or father can include the effects of mothering or fathering on children's lives. What it means to be a diabetic can include how diabetics consider their diet.

I have officially been a teacher since 1970 when I received my B.A. in English from the University of Wisconsin and became a middle school reading and English teacher in Matawan, N.J. Thirty-three and a half years and two degrees later, I have now taught senior citizens, pre-schoolers, parent volunteers, adult learners, teachers-in-training, high school and college students, as well as my own two children and my husband's office staff. I might decide it's finally time to define the role of teacher. I would include as my list of distinguishing characteristics an absolute respect for the intelligence of others, a perception that the medium is the message (Marshall McLuhan), and a willingness to laugh at oneself and avoid the perfectionism which blocks learning. I could contrast these characteristics with qualities I believe have no place in teaching: believing that one knows more because one is older or the teacher, believing that saying something equals doing it, and believing that stern seriousness and hiding one's own mistakes maintains standards necessary for learning. I could further define my idea of what constitutes a teacher with stories from my classrooms. I could compare how I was taught to teach with how I have learned to teach. I could show the effects of my teaching on students, and I could show the effects of my students on my teaching.

Ask the "write" question for your definition personal essay this way: "What role do I play in life that I can name and describe?" Begin by thinking about what people call you—a grandfather, a widow, a transactional analyst, a biker, a golfer, a pool shark, a professional volunteer.

If you have a writing area in mind, insert it into the question like this, "What am I called as a consequence of (to use our examples once again) divorcing, parenting, visiting a new country, fighting in a war, or coping with an illness? What do I want to describe about what lies beneath this label of divorcee, single parent, tourist, veteran, or Parkinsonian?

Before you answer the "write" question, though, look ahead to the example definition essays.

Example Definition Essays

In the following example essay, Janis Jaquith defines Attention Deficit Disorder by describing her behavior at various ages and showing what she makes of the world's sensory stimulation. The examples are arranged chronologically covering early childhood and grade school. The narrative and descriptive details provide examples of the symptoms that characterize the behavior and thinking of children with Attention Deficit Disorder. Reading the author's account of her behavior at home and at school, we start to understand the way it functions for the person with Attention Deficit and how that person really doesn't think of it as inappropriate.

As you read, think about the other techniques the author uses to define Attention Deficit Disorder. Note the how-to, comparison and contrast, division and classification, and cause and effect in addition to description and narration.

When you are done reading the essay, imagine who might benefit from reading this extended definition essay as a way of learning about this oft-mentioned condition.

The View From In Here

(What Attention Deficit Disorder Feels Like)

I'm lying on my back in the sunshine, holding my little pink elephant up against the clouds — pretending that we're flying — when a shadow falls over me. It's my grandfather. He brings his face closer, right into my playpen, and he's smiling and saying something to me, something sing-songy. I turn away from him, hoping he'll just go away. This playpen is mine. When I'm in here nobody bothers me. I get to think and do anything I please. My grandfather goes away and now I can get back to flying with my elephant.

I hear my father's voice. He's home from work. I run to my hiding place, a new one. I try not to giggle and give myself away as my father looks for me, saying, "Where's my little girl? Where's my Janny?" This is my best hiding place yet. I'm in the bathroom, buried under laundry in the clothes hamper. My hiding place is too good, and eventually, Daddy gives up.

I decide that I sort of like it in the laundry hamper. It smells funny, but I like the way it muffles sound. My father's voice sounded far away, and now I should be able to hear my parents talking as they sit down at the kitchen table for their daily cocktail. But I hear nothing. And I like it.

I'm sitting at a desk in first grade. The teacher is standing up in front of us, and she's talking and talking about something or other. Her glasses are hanging from a chain around her neck. Like a necklace, but not really. She's wearing one of those big fake roses, it's pinned to her dress. I think my grandmother has one of those.

I look down at my desk and there are all these little squares of green paper. I don't know where they came from. Each square has a number on it. What am I supposed to do with those? I look around at the other kids and a hot stab of panic shoots through my chest. All the other kids are doing something special with those numbers. They all know what to do. Now the teacher is moving up and down the aisles, licking little gold stars and pressing them to the foreheads of the kids who know what they are doing. She goes right past me.

I don't belong here. I don't know how I got here. I don't know what I'm supposed to do. I'd go home . . . but I don't know how to do that, either.

&

First grade is better now. I know where everything is. When I get here in the morning, I know where to hang up my coat, I know where Mrs. Prolman keeps the paper and where to find a box of those terrific fat red pencils. I feel like I belong here. Best of all, I know right where my desk is.

Reading group is wonderful. I'm very good at it, it turns out. When it's my turn to read, everyone is quiet and I can read aloud perfectly, faster than anyone else.

But now, reading group is over and we're back at our seats. Now I have to take out my *Think and Do* book. That's the workbook that goes with those Dick, Jane and Sally stories. I try to tell people how much I hate this stupid *Think and Do* workbook, but nobody listens to me, nobody cares about how much I hate to do this workbook.

I know the story, okay? I read it. I got it. So why do I have to answer questions about it in this stupid workbook? I try to write the answers, but my letters come out all wrong and so I erase and it leaves a messy smudge so I erase harder and make a hole in the page. It's like this for every answer, just about, and on every page. Sometimes I tell Mrs. Prolman I can't find my workbook, or I hide it over on the bookshelves. But she always finds it. I stare at the page with its gray smudges and holes and I imagine striking a match and burning it up right there on my desk.

Trying to do what I'm supposed to do in this workbook is like when my father sits down at the kitchen table to figure out his taxes; that's what it's like. Or when my mother sits in that same chair, doing stuff with her checkbook and bills and then she stops and buries her face in both her hands. It's like that. . . . Only every day.

I'm in third grade, and do I ever love the setup in this classroom. It's a real old school and the desks and chairs are screwed into the floor. The rows stay straight all the time. I love this. And in the back of the classroom is a bookshelf with a collection of books that are like fifth or sixth grade reading level. If I get my work done, I can go back there and read anything I want, and I don't have to answer any stupid questions about it. Pure joy.

I just got off the bus, came in and hung up my raincoat. I settle into my seat when I look up at the side blackboard. Oh, no. There's before-school work on the board. This is as unfair as anything I can think of. BEFORE school work? Give me a break. Let me catch my breath, for heaven's sake. I take a good look at it and feel the bottom drop out of my stomach: It's a word problem, with pints and quarts and gallons. Oh, my God. I don't know which way is up. I take out a piece of paper and at least write my name on it. Mrs. Donahue is going to call me a featherhead again, I'm sure of it. I don't know where to start. I don't know how to think about this problem. And she has explained this stuff to us over and over.

What if I'm retarded? I hope they don't put me in special class. I will die if they put me in special class.

৯৯

For the zillionth time, Mrs. Donahue is at the front of the class, explaining about pints and quarts and gallons. She's doing the problem that was on the side board this morning. I am trying so hard to pay attention, it practically hurts. I say to myself: try try try. But trying to pay attention feels like I'm trying to hold a beach ball under water. The effort is too great, and it feels so unnatural.

I'm sorry, everybody, but I just can't do it. I allow the beach ball to pop up into its own realm, where it belongs. What a relief!

Mrs. Donahue's voice sounds far away now, a kind of honking music with its own rising and falling rhythm. When she moves her mouth, there are all these little wrinkles that radiate out from her lips, especially the top one.

All this talk about pints and gallons makes me think about chocolate milk. The way it's so thick and tastes so good. I wonder what it would taste like if I put chocolate milk on my sugar crisp in the morning.

From somewhere far away, I hear my name. Ah, jeez. How did she know I wasn't listening? I was looking right at her. So, what's the answer, she wants to know? Everyone's looking at me and smirking, including Mrs. Donahue. The answer must be ridiculously obvious to any normal person. The boy behind me whispers, "retard" and I will myself to die.

৯৯

It's morning. I'm sitting on the floor of my room, feeling a little chilly, in just my underwear. I'm stacking up my glossy encyclopedias, fanning them outward until they look like a sweeping, fancy staircase, the kind Cinderella ran down. I think it looks really good.

My mother comes to the door. She looks like she's crazy. Her face is all twisted and mad. She sounds like she's strangling when she says, "The bus comes in five minutes. You have been in here for half an hour. What have you been doing?" Half an hour? That sounds improbable to me. It feels like about three minutes.

❧

I'm standing at the bottom of Vonnie Erickson's back porch. Vonnie is a year older than me, and I really want her to be my friend. I'm not sure how to go about this friend acquisition thing, so I figure persistence is my best bet. She's at her kitchen window, saying, "No! I don't want to come out and play with you!" "Are you sure?" I say for perhaps the twentieth time. Vonnie's face disappears from the window. Somehow, I can't seem to shut up. "Honest and truly?" I say. From somewhere in the kitchen I hear her say, "Yes!" "Bably and Booly?" I cleverly reply. Her face appears again, just long enough to shut the window. Oh, well. I had a pretty good idea that I was being obnoxious, but I didn't know how else to be. I couldn't stop myself. I would have used another script, if I'd had one. Persistence usually pays off with my parents and brother and sister. They'll do most anything to get me to shut the hell up, as my big brother says. He's in college.

❧

I'm in fourth grade and the difference between my smart side and dumb side is getting bigger all the time. I'm one of the best readers and we've been writing these stories lately and we are allowed to just make things up and write about them. Just make things up! This is great.

What's not so great is that I get marked down because my handwriting is so bad. It's not like Mr. Sweeney can't read it, because he can, and he really likes my stories, but he puts me down a whole grade because he says it looks like I wrote it with my foot instead of my hand.

I try, I really do, but my pencil just will not do what I tell it to do. It's like everyone else is some kind of super duper artist, capturing these letters and words on paper, and I can't even draw a straight line. All anyone says about my handwriting is: if you'd just be more careful. If you'd just slow down. If you'd just try. Like, if I was a better person, I'd have better penmanship.

I look at other kids' handwriting and I think: How do they DO it?

❧

Just the sight of math paper makes me sick to my stomach. It's small and beige and it's flecked with tiny woody bits. If you don't think about what it's for, you might actually like math paper. There are no lines so it would be great for drawing on, or folding into something neat. By the time I'm finished with it, though, you wouldn't want to even look at it.

We're supposed to be real whizzes at long division by fourth grade, but I can't even line up the numbers on top of each other to make a column, and I end up adding the wrong stuff together. Being stuck in the middle of one of those problems is like being lost in a department store when you're little. There's no way you're getting out of it by yourself. It's hopeless.

❧

For years, or since first grade, anyway, I have enjoyed many happy hours sitting in boxes. You know, those big ones that TVs or whatever come in. Give me a box, a light and a book and I'll be happy for hours. Now, does that sound weird to you? I don't think so.

When we get a good box, I go down to the cellar where we keep the Christmas decorations, and I get the cord and bulb that go into our light-up snowman. You can just twist it right out and use that light any way you want to.

I make a hole in the top of the box and drop that light bulb down into it. I use one of those aluminum foil chicken pot pie plates for a shade. Just poke a hole in that, too. I crawl in the box through the flaps, which I have on one end, and I just pull the flaps up, and there I am! This is the best place to be. You can read, or draw or just think straight—which is great.

Well, my mother thinks I'm nuts. She worries about me sitting in the box all the time. A few weeks ago, she took me to the doctor's office, she was so worried. It wasn't even time for a check-up or shots or anything.

So, Dr. MacDougall puts me on the scale and takes my blood pressure, looks in my ears and all that jazz. My mother's watching the whole thing, like Dr. MacDougall is gonna find something in my ear that will explain why I like to sit in the box. When he's done, my mother says, "Well?" And Dr. MacDougall shrugs his shoulders and says, "If she wants to sit in the box, let her sit in the box."

Anyway, the box mysteriously disappeared a few days later, so I had to move into the closet. My sister (she's in high school) is ready to kill me. She says it's her closet too and I ruin all her clothes by squishing them all to one side of the closet. Like I care. I have a clubhouse in that closet. The walls in there are this wonderful, smooth white plaster. It's great for writing on. On the wall, I wrote down all the different jobs in the club, you know, president, treasurer, secretary, members . . . And then I filled in my name under each one. I get along very well with everyone in the club.

My fifth-grade classroom is a nightmare. The desks are all over the place. Nothing is nailed into the floor, and I never know what the place is gonna look like from one day to the next. I hate this. It makes me feel like I'm mentally ill, or something. I just get so confused that it's hard to think about anything else. Mr. Fratianni — he's my teacher — he likes to change the place around all the time, and it drives me crazy, I mean it. How would he like it if his wife rearranged the kitchen all the time? It would be hard to get anything done in there, wouldn't it? He'd never know where anything was.

Today, Mr. Fratianni had us in groups of four, four desks all pushed together and facing each other. Actually I kind of like this most of the time, because there's always someone to talk to or poke or make goofy drawings for when things get boring, which is most of the time. I don't get much work done, but I'm having a good time.

‚ôä

As it happens, I'm in the principal's office right now. I have to stand with my back right next to, but not touching, the side of a file cabinet. I have to stay here until recess is over. This is humiliating.

Here's what happened: I was at my lunch table in the cafeteria, sitting next to Claire Fogg. Claire finishes her hard-boiled egg, which stunk, by the way, and she takes out a Hershey bar for dessert. It just so happens that I am crazy about Hershey bars. I watch her slide that long silver rectangle out from the brown paper sleeve and then she opens it up, and I can smell it.

It's the kind of Hershey bar that has the little lines pressed into it, so you can, like, share it easily. Claire breaks off about a third of it, when she looks up at me watching her. She gets this squinty look in her eyes and just shakes her head, as if to say: Forget it. I'm not sharing this with anyone. The next thing I know, the rest of that Hershey bar is in my mouth, all of it. And it is so good, you wouldn't believe it.

And then, Claire is yelling and fake-crying and it turns out that there was a teacher who saw the whole thing. All the teacher kept saying was, "What were you thinking? Why did you do that?"

I couldn't explain it to her, but the truth is, there was no thinking part. I went right from wanting that candy bar to chewing it. Boom. I don't know what happened to the part where I was supposed to consider whether to do it or not.

This happens to me all the time. I call out answers and questions in class when it's not time to. I interrupt like crazy, even when I don't want to. Other people don't do this, and it makes me wonder how they know when it's the right time to speak up, because I know that if I don't say what's on my mind right away, I'll forget it. And sometimes the ideas are jumping into my mind so fast, it's like popcorn popping. And I don't know which idea to say out loud first. They all seem important. So, I'll end up blurting out something that isn't really what I wanted to say at all.

Which drives me crazy. And while I'm on the subject of memory, I don't know how other kids always seem to bring the right books home for homework, and then they actually get it all done, AND they can find it the next day. This amazes me. It's like the handwriting thing, I guess. Just another talent that I don't have.

❧

I'm pretty sure now that I'm not retarded, but I wonder if I'm going senile. I'm serious. Is that possible in fifth grade? I read about lots of weird diseases every month in *Reader's Digest*, and I wonder if I have some of those diseases, like being senile. I'm always forgetting things and nobody believes me. They say I do it for attention. Yeah, right. Like I need more attention. I'll forget my homework, I'll forget where I took off one of my shoes, I'll forget to come home . . .

And to show you how messed up I really am, I'll remember something one day, forget it the next, and then remember it the third day! Like, if you asked me right now what nine times eight is, I really couldn't tell you. But I knew it yesterday, and chances are it'll come back to me tomorrow. If that's not senile, I don't know what is . . . .

Anyway, one good thing about standing here all alone in the principal's office is I have all this free time to think straight.

Not such a bad deal, for a weirdo like me.

How the Writer Makes a Discovery and Shares It in "The View from in Here"

Janis Jaquith details her sensory response to the world, her actions, her questions, and her behaviors. Within her description and narration, she lets readers in on why some things are appealing to her and others offensive and how she copes in a world that doesn't recognize how its actions and environments affect a nervous system like hers. These vignettes add up to demonstrate the characteristics of a person with Attention Deficit Disorder—sensory peculiarities, frustration, lack of small motor skills, impulsivity, annoying persistence, impatience, social inappropriateness, panic at not understanding situations and directions, and understanding that others are working on a different wave length and not knowing how to get in sync. Jaquith lets us know the ways in which the responses of others do not help her understand her problem (a failure in cause and effect) and how she looks for answers herself in what she reads. Reading about senility, for example, she applies what she's read to the way her mind works. Readers know she can't be senile and empathize with her need to find out what the matter is.

Because it establishes empathy, her definition helps readers discover her truth—the unusual behavior of kids with Attention Deficit Disorder is upsetting to those around them. However, it is also mysterious and difficult for the one with the condition, often in ways others do not recognize. By ending with her happiness at standing alone in the principal's office, Jaquith shows both herself and her reader just how important moment-by-moment calming of the distracted brain is and how this happiness at having a moment's peace outweighs any fear of repercussions to come.

Following is another definition essay. I wrote it to define the working writer in each of us. I did the clustering exercise using the word "role," and I came up with types of working writers, including the "blocked writer" and the "unblocked writer." I had been considering, for my students who were having trouble getting started on essays how the writer self is actually with us even when we are not writing. I wondered if I could write an essay defining that working but unseen writer self.

Let Your Writer Self Be With You

"Issues of productivity," "sitting still with loneliness and bore-dom," "compartments of time." I mulled these phrases over. A close writing colleague was suffering from writer's block and had written them to me in a letter. As I thought about what I consider the source of writer's block, I dialed my cousin. I often make phone calls while I am thinking about things that I don't have answers for.

She was busy—"I have twelve cakes in the oven," she said, "Can you believe it?" In addition, her two single young adult children were visiting from other cities, and needing to move, she was look-ing for a new apartment. Wow, I thought, that's a lot.

Then I considered my husband, who was busy writing two arti-cles at once for a technical journal. He had taken me to a movie the evening before because he couldn't get anywhere in his writ-ing. Mulling over both my husband's and my cousin's projects, I realized something about my own approach to creating. I had made six kinds of soup from scratch in the last two weeks since I started teaching several days a week, because I need to do some-thing while I worry about what I will say to my students.

Each of us bakes our creative cakes so differently. My husband walks away from the cakes, hoping that once he is away from them, they'll continue to cook somewhere deep inside of him. Sure enough, after we'd eaten a quick teriyaki meal and drunk a cup of coffee and taken our seats in the theater, the "aha hit." Not only did he know what was at the root of his articles' problems, he realized his new understanding meant he wouldn't have to start over. Boy, he enjoyed that movie! But he would have anyway, even if the "aha" was delayed. He counts on it arriving sometime. There's always HBO waiting at home until the moment strikes.

My cousin—well, her cakes are for real—she's a health food chef and teacher and an allergy-free dessert specialist. She'll keep right on putting those babies in and out of the oven and publish-ing her recipes in *Vegetarian Times*. Sometimes she makes mistakes that lead to treasured discoveries. Recently, when she reached for rice cereal instead of flour, she decided to bake the cake using it! Later, she watched her guests put their first forkfuls into their mouths. They thought the cake was delicious and she had a new wheat-free dessert.

I group things. I was teaching so the writing was on the back burner and I got into my domestic chores between classes. After the quarter, when the courses were done for a stretch, I'd be writing up a storm, the frozen food I'd stored in my freezer decreasing daily.

I am a user of "compartments of time," but my cousin and my husband use "currents of time" and notice the little surprises that bob up and down in them.

I don't know, if you are like them or me or someone else, dear reader, but let me propose something for those of you who need to get over writer's block, severe or mild. My suggestion comes from reading *Who's Writing This?*, edited by Anteaus literary magazine editor Daniel Halpern. It is a collection of essays by 50 writers and poets on writing and writers block published by The Ecco Press in 1994. Halpern had entreated contributors to respond to Jorge Luis Borges' statement, "It is to my other self, to Borges, that things happen."

Reading this, I began to imagine the writer in me as a separate being from the me who has been going, doing, bitching, wishing to own things and making plans. If Bender is my self to whom things happen, then maybe my writing voice, which is the self to whom things don't happen, has some nice insight as an observer on what is happening to Bender and whatever it is that distracts her from the writer's work and voice.

But how does this writer person, the one to whom things have not happened, the one that doesn't have cakes in the oven, the one who chooses the batter of the written word over and over again, get through to me, the one who owns the computer?

I continued mulling this over for a few days as I taught and did chores. When my husband again asked me to go see a movie, I said no because I was going to make soup. While I chopped, I found that the rhythm of chopping all those vegetables occupied the Bender to whom things happen and made the writer inside of her, the one to whom things do not happen, think about things. She was remembering a lot. She remembered events like the time her mother cut a finger badly just as her dad came home from a week on the road as a traveling salesman, and she remembered planting a vegetable garden one summer. She remembered her son's quails laying eggs in a cage just to the side of the garden. The one to whom things does not happen remembered the way Bender's husband buys beets of many colors and roasts them in the oven. She thought of the way Bender's daughter stuffs artichokes with cloves of garlic and puts lemon juice in the pot of water she boils them in, thereby refining a family favorite. As Bender chopped vegetables, the one to whom things do not happen was chopping the events of Bender's life into images that delight or concern or make Bender cry. She thought of the day the quail were eaten by a raccoon and a friend said, "Of course, they were helpless prey, unable to escape the cage. She thought of how she could use this newly surfaced thought to write about something important to find out about, something about how what nourished Bender's son with its eggs and beauty was lost because it was captive to a family that didn't know how to protect it. She will learn how much sorrow Bender holds knowing this is true for so much besides the quail of long ago. As the soup simmered, Bender was sitting down and the one to whom things don't happen was getting words on a page.

I believe that when we are stuck, if we can adopt a rhythmic action like running, shooting baskets, cooking, dancing, swimming, or bicycle riding, the writer in us will separate from our life's doings and burst into words. If we concentrate on the rhythmic action, the one inside to whom things do not happen, the writing and observing person, will make images surface. If the one who is doing allows the images to register, the one who is doing will sit down and the one who writes will write!

How the Writer Makes a Discovery and Shares It in " Let Your Writer Self Be With You "

Utilizing bits of dialog from a note I received, I ponder the words of a colleague wondering about a solution to her writer's block. I use a how-to pattern as a way of driving my essay forward when I reveal that I make phone calls when I do not have an answer to a problem. I call a cousin and finding her in the act of creating, consider her methods to define creativity. I think about my husband's ways since he is writing, and I think of my own. I do this with narration. Then, I name the characteristics of our styles and use metaphor to evoke them more fully. Then I try an experiment. I incorporate something that I read into my thinking and experience the results. In describing the process, I use a how-to pattern of thinking.

Satisfied that I have found a way to contact the writer who is always with us, I offer instruction for others so they can find and hear the writer within. In looking for a way to help others with writer's block, I found that I could write during my traditionally non-writing time, and I hope in the essay that others will give the method a try and make a similar discovery.

Next, consider an exercise to facilitate your extended definition writing.

Exercise for Developing Your Material

A Dictionary Game Look Alike

Play the following game with your family or a group of four or five people. It is fun even for those who are not going to write a definition essay.

Everyone writes one word on a scrap of paper, a word they believe no one in the room has heard. The word can be a nickname or a word coined by friends. It can be an esoteric term from a hobby or course of study. It can be a foreign word. The word, however, mustn't be spelled exactly the same as another word someone might know. For instance, the word "crunchy" can mean embarrassing in school-age slang and also traditionally describes texture or sound (crunchy snacks and crunchy snow). This word would not be a good candidate for the game because the person defining "crunchy" would already know the traditional meaning even if he or she didn't know the slang meaning.

When all have written down words, have them fold up the papers and drop them into a hat or bowl. Everyone now draws a paper out of the hat or bowl. If anyone picks up a word he or she put in, have that person pick again. When all have selected words for which they do not know the meaning, have everyone write for five minutes, making up definitions for these words.

For instance, if I had picked the word "hoila hoila," I might write:

This is a phrase a community of descendants of explorers from the South Pacific use to express their shock and surprise when a member of their community marries outside of the clan. For example, one might hear: Hoila Hoila Marie has not called her mother in ten years, or her grandson went hoila hoila on her and lives in California.

When everyone in the group has written a "definition," the group listens to each word and "definition." After each reader, the person who contributed the word can explain its "real" meaning. I might find out, for instance, that hoila hoila is the sound a group member's children made when she served them food they thought was too fancy.

After you have heard all the words and their new and original meanings, think about all the techniques used in defining them. I am sure that the people in your group wrote, just as I did, about the class of activities, events, people, or objects to which their word belonged. I am sure they described how the activity, event, person, or object is distinguished by its main characteristics or functions. Some people may have included examples. Some may have compared or contrasted their object, event, or activity to other objects, events, or activities. Others may have told what characteristics their word did not include as a way of honing in on a meaning.

We use these techniques of defining quite naturally. Noticing them in the game will help you feel confident in your ability to write an extended definition essay.

If you can't do this exercise with a group of people, go to a library or newsstand and pick up reading material in Italian, French, or Spanish. Jot down some words and take them home. Put each foreign word at the top of a page. Next, write a few paragraphs for each word, "defining" it based on how it sounds to you and what you associate with the sound. You can also take words from law books, medical books, or technical manuals, as long as the words you choose don't have exact homonyms in everyday speech.

Exercises for Locating Your Definition Material

Put the word "role" in the middle of a piece of paper. Then cluster around it all the roles you can think of, the ones you like, the ones you don't like, the ones you envy in other people's lives, and the ones you regret in your life or in another person's life. You may come up with employee of the year, youngest sibling, non-custodial parent, rock-band leader, aspiring musician, or gossip.

You may not have a name yet for a role you could write about; perhaps you have just a feeling. Write that feeling and then cluster labels around it. For instance, perhaps you felt "out of it" in high school. Write that down and circle it. Then think up labels in high school that contributed to that feeling: class valedictorian, class clown, nerd, slower learner, pot-head, member of the "wrong side of the tracks" crowd.

When you find a role that interests you, do another cluster around that word in the middle of your paper. You might write about a condition you have or someone close to you has that requires special care. If you are diabetic, for instance, you might see that many people think that being one means only taking insulin and not eating sugar. You know, though, that having and managing diabetes entails far more. Ask yourself five questions: "What are the characteristics of this role I play or used to play?" "What are the things this role is not?" "How does one perform this role?" "How is this role different from other roles or different from what other people may think?" "Why do I call it what I do?" If it helps, cluster answers for each of the questions.

If the word "role" doesn't grab you, use the word "situation" and think of situations you or people close to you find themselves in—homelessness, having chemotherapy, living with a cancer patient, being an "ex." When you have decided on one situation that interests you, do another cluster using that word. Ask yourself: "What are the characteristics of this situation?" "What is missing in this situation?" "How does one behave in this situation?" "How is one restricted from behaving in this situation?"

If you already have a topic in mind, ask the "write" question this way: "What am I called as a consequence of _____(insert your writing area)? If, for instance, your area is fighting in a war, you may have come up with veteran, hero, coward, sergeant, private, or general. Chose the role that interests you. Then use the questions from above and cluster around the word you have selected.

Writing the Definition Essay

When you are finished clustering, do a freewrite. Write about the role you are describing by remembering the way definitions worked in the group game. Feel free to go from one definition technique to another: listing the characteristics involved, listing the characteristics that are not involved, comparing and contrasting characteristics, using narratives as example and discussing functions. This will help you extend your definition of the role you are exploring. Put the freewrite away for a bit. Look at it again. Read it over and see what interests you in the writing.

When you feel ready, start the first draft of your definition personal essay. You might start with an anecdote about yourself or someone you know who performs in the role you are defining. Or you might start with a dictionary definition to which you will add or with which you might disagree. You can plunge right into the classification and characteristics you have distinguished and want to discuss. You might quote dialog from someone who thinks of you in the role you are describing or reproduce dialog that irritates you because of what you know.

Developing a Draft

Your first-hand experience with a subject puts you in a better position than most to define it. If you have recently been in a hospital, you know the role "patient" better than those who haven't been one. If you have just seen your last child off to college, you know what "an empty nest" is better than those who haven't yet experienced it. If you are a community activist or a welfare mother, a plumber or someone with Epstein-Barr Syndrome, you know more about these roles and situations than others do. Define them and learn the truth of your experience while educating others.

When you have gotten from a beginning to an ending, read your essay to your trusted listeners. When they tell you what stuck with them, what they felt when listening and where they are curious to know more, you will have important information to help you continue drafting. Most of us don't put enough detail and examples in our first drafts or recognize just how interesting our take on the role is to those who are listening. If the responses indicate that this is so, cluster again around the role you are taking on and see if you can find more detail, examples, and anecdotes to include in your essay. Perhaps you need to show how us how something to do with the role is made or done. See if comparing what you are doing in this role to what others think you are doing helps make the essay full. Extend yourself on the page and offer the experience that has brought you knowledge.

Chapter X

The Argument and Persuasion Essay

Write Question #8: In what area do I have experience that can inform others and change their thinking or actions?

> *. . . reason works better when emotions are present . . .*
> —Rollo May, *The Courage to Create*

There are times in your life when you desire to persuade others to take action or change their thinking. Letters to the editor and op-ed sections of newspapers and magazines contain writings from personal experience motivated in this way.

What does it take to write persuasively and to move others to read and stay interested in your argument and point of view and perhaps change their thinking and behavior? There is a recipe to this kind of writing. The ingredients, mixed in a variety of orders include: 1) making an assertion; 2) providing at least three supports; 3) ordering that support toward a crescendo; 4) giving time to the opposing position; and 5) using images and details to persuade the reader instead of relying on emotionally loaded words that tell, rather than show.

It probably will not surprise you that the ingredients you'll use in the above recipe include any and all of the previous seven essay styles.

Eda La Shan, the early childhood specialist, once said something about dealing with children that I always remember when writing argument and persuasion essays. She said that children and adults are most alike in their feelings and least alike in their thinking.

I think there are parallels between the ways many of us talk to children and the ways we approach our persuasive writing. How often we tell children to calm down and behave without finding out what they are feeling that is causing them to fidget or to whine. If we start first with identifying feelings ("What is troubling you?"), and we address those feelings ("Yes, it must be uncomfortable to sit here when your feet don't reach the floor."), then we can "fix" the situation ("Here, I'll move over. Why don't you put your legs up on the seat for a while?").

In essay writing, this need to address feelings before presenting solutions translates into two ideas. First, to write effective argument and persuasion pieces, you must understand the feelings that make your opponents behave as they do, and you must express that understanding. Second, revealing your own feelings is the best way to make connection with your readers—although they may not think like you do, they do have the same repertoire of feelings, just as adults understand discomfort even if the situations that make them uncomfortable are different than the ones that make children uncomfortable.

"Growing up in the U.S. makes one predisposed to cultural arrogance, a sense that our culture is not only different but better than others, a belief that everyone else should speak English but that it is not necessary for us to speak their languages," wrote Alan Guskin, President of Antioch University, in the Fall, 1991 issue of *The Antiochian*. This very predisposition is so internalized that even inside our country, inside our own families, we are unaware of how this "cultural snobbism" blocks effective communication. This predisposition diminishes our ability to consider other people's points of view, the validity and historical roots of their views. We might not even recognize there is room for these differences. In addition, sometimes we don't know if our point of view is obtained through our own experience, or whether it is an untested, unverified, soaked-in-by-osmosis piece of cultural snobbism.

The points of view you can most persuasively argue and present in the hopes of having others understand come directly from your experience. If you have lived something, you are an authority. But you must examine your experience closely to find out what you have really come to believe. The argument and persuasion essay provides a strategy for accomplishing this. First you reveal your beliefs, and then you open the door for another to go your way if they are willing.

Examining your experience in the argument and persuasion essay, you learn not only what your own point of view is, but also how you formed it. If you begin by believing that everyone (including yourself) should think like you do and value what you value, you will short circuit your own ability to find out what you really believe and what you truly value. In working the steps and exercises I am about to describe, you will have the opportunity to learn about your own thinking and where it came from. You will get to see if it still fits.

The "write" question for this essay style is, "In what area do I have experience that can inform others and change their thinking or actions?" If you have a topic in mind, insert it into the "write" question: In what area of, to use our trusty examples, divorcing, parenting, visiting, fighting wars, or coping with illness do I have experience that can inform others and change their thinking or actions? After we consider the sample essays in this chapter, I will share a way of mining areas of your experience to find many topics that you can write persuasively about, perhaps more than you believe possible. Using personal experience in persuasive writing provides material you can use to persuade others. It also helps you use feelings to encourage the reader to understand the importance of your argument.

Example Argument and Persuasion Essays

Linda Kulp uses her personal experience to convince others to change their behavior and their thinking about a particular type of anxiety. She wants to persuade her readers to help others rather than dismiss their worries. As you read her essay, pay attention to the ways she sways your opinion. Pay attention, also, to which of the previous seven essay styles she employs. Do you see the strength of the description, narration, comparison and contrast, how-to, and cause and effect styles she uses?

Generalized Anxiety Disorder (GAD), A Real Illness

The light is green, but my foot remains anchored against the brake. Cars coming from the opposing lane fly by leaving occasional brief opportunities to cross the highway. Behind me in a red pick-up, a middle-aged man hangs out of the window yelling at me, "Go, you Idiot! What the hell you waiting for?" Horns wail from a growing line-up in the turn lane. Still, I cannot move.

Tears blur my vision as I glance down at the hand-drawn map on the passenger seat. This is where I'm supposed to turn. I know it, but everything's moving so fast, everything, except me. My hands grip the wheel; still I cannot move.

Questions race through my brain: What if I don't make it across? What if I get hit? What will happen to my two young sons in the backseat? What if they die? What if I cause someone else to die? What if . . .. The light changes to yellow, then red. I take a breath knowing it will soon be green again, and I will have to move. A sharp pain digs a path through my chest; my body is trembling. I want to disappear as the name-calling and cussing from the unfortunate drivers behind me grow louder. "Oh God, help me. Please help me."

Green light. Suddenly, without thinking, I feel my foot jump from the brake and floor the accelerator. I make the turn crossing the highway narrowly missing an oncoming station wagon. I'm on automatic now, not thinking, just driving.

Home, I tell my husband what happened. "You just have to learn to be more aggressive when you're driving; you're such a worrier!" he quips, brushing off my fears once again. He wants to help, but he doesn't understand that what I'm experiencing goes much deeper than just being afraid to drive new places. He doesn't understand my constant worrying, my need to be perfect, and my feelings of being disconnected from the people closest to me. I want to explain it all to him, but what's happening to me is a mystery I can't unravel.

Well-meaning friends and family tell me to just relax and stop worrying. Sometimes they make fun of my fears without realizing how difficult it is for me to control them. They think I'm just an obsessive worrier who needs to "chill out." Comments meant to show me how unrealistic my fears are such as, "You're crazy to worry about that," and "What do you mean you're afraid to drive on the highway? That's the silliest thing I've ever heard," only confirm my inadequacies.

I don't know when I became "such a worrier." As a child, I cared about the things most kids do: having friends, doing well in school, etc.; but I don't remember experiencing any long-term anxiety over things. As I moved into my teen years, my worrying increased as my mother began drinking more heavily. Weighted with the responsibilities of caring for my younger siblings, high school, and working part-time to help support the family, I began to withdraw from friendships and outside activities.

I married a man who was very protective of me and very good at taking care of things. After our sons were born, he encouraged me to work at home. For the next ten years I worked at home, took care of the house, and raised my sons. I seldom drove anywhere except to the grocery store or library in the small town we lived in. In the safety of our home, I had little to fear.

Then, my husband, at age 38, had a heart attack. No longer could I avoid driving in the city, going out at night alone, or getting a job outside the home that paid enough to support our family. I held on by telling myself that as soon as my husband recovered things would get back to normal, but they never did. My husband changed after his heart attack. He felt he might not always be around to take care of me and began pushing me to be more independent. The more he pushed, the more my anxiety grew. I began experiencing panic attacks and drowning in dark pools of depression.

Fear and anxiety had cost me many workdays. I literally worried myself sick to the point where I lacked the energy to function. At my husband's request, I continued to work outside the home, but I didn't apply for promotions because I was afraid of change, and I worried I'd have to drive to a meeting someplace I'd never been, or that I my supervisor would discover that I really wasn't all that good at my job.

I kept telling myself that I could find the answers I needed if I worked hard enough. I read self-help book after self-help book on how to have confidence, how to be happy, how to stop worrying, how to be a better parent, a better wife, a better person. I tried positive self-talk, talking to other "worriers," self-medicating with herbs, but nothing worked for long. With each failure, my self-esteem took a nose-dive and my hope of being "normal" began to fade. When I saw signs that my youngest son was becoming a worrier like me, I decided to seek help from my primary care physician. I had to find out what was wrong with me in order to be able to help my son.

I was diagnosed with General Anxiety Disorder (GAD). GAD is a condition that affects more than 4 million adults in the U.S. I was relieved to discover that anxiety disorders are treatable through a regiment of medication, counseling, nutrition, and exercise. Although finding the right medication is frustrating and can take time, after several years, I believe I've found the antidepressant that works best for me. I could accept the challenge of learning to exercise more and eat nutritionally, but the need for counseling embarrassed me and I didn't go for any.

The depression that often accompanies anxiety disorders further strained my relationship with my husband. Years of struggling with my anxiety and my husband's frustration over why I wasn't "getting better" caused us to spend less and less time together until, finally, my husband asked for a divorce. Once again, I was drowning in anxiety. That's when I reluctantly went into counseling with a physician-referred specialist in anxiety disorders. She taught me relaxation techniques and strategies for dealing with worry.

Although my counselor's help, support, and knowledge were pivotal, it would have been very helpful if people understood that GAD is a real illness, often hereditary, like diabetes or heart disease and that anxiety can be just as crippling as losing a limb. Just because they cannot see the handicap, doesn't mean it isn't real. I believe that the support of family and friends is vital to the recovery process. First of all, friends, family and coworkers can help those of us suffering from GAD by acknowledging the hard work it takes to get better and that recovery is often slow with setbacks along the way. Here are some other things loved ones can do:

+ Be a patient listener. Allow us to talk about our fears. I was often too ashamed to discuss my fears with my husband, and I thought he wouldn't take them seriously. I'm now in a relationship with a man who encourages me to talk to him about my worries. By attending several counseling sessions with me, he learned the importance of "talk therapy" and sometimes, just having an understanding listener eases anxiety.
+ Help us to recognize times when we worry about imagined "what if" scenarios. When a GAD sufferer begins with the "what ifs," try to rationalize his/her fears by asking, "How likely do you think that is to happen?" Fear has a way of

running away with one's imagination. When my imagination runs wild with worry, I call my sister who calmly gives me the reassurance I need to get through the situation.

+ Praise us for small accomplishments in our recovery. After my divorce, I moved to a new town. I was terrified to drive to the mall alone. A close friend drove me there a few times, and then rode along with me as I drove to the mall. He praised me continually for knowing which way to turn, merging into traffic, and staying focused on my driving until I felt I could do it on my own. My sons are my greatest source of inspiration and praise. Although they are grown, they take time to email me the same kind of encouraging little notes I used to put in their lunchboxes when they were small. No matter what else is happening, those little emails make a difference!

+ Learn all you can about the disorder and the situations that often "trigger" an attack. Different things can trigger an attack of fear and panic. Some of my "triggers" are: driving to new places, driving after dark, new social situations, pressure to perform a new task, and comments by others that cause me to feel unworthy of being loved.

+ Realize that GAD is a real illness that often stems from a chemical imbalance in the body, which requires medication. Worrying runs in my family. My grandfather worried about the house catching on fire to the point of checking the burners on the stove over and over before he went to bed. My mother took "nerve medicine" for years. It was a family secret that no one discussed. Two of my three sisters are on anti-anxiety medications, and at least one of my sons exhibits signs that he may have inherited GAD. So far, my son has been able to control his anxiety without medication but instead through a regiment of nutrition, exercise, stress management, and family support. We've come a long way, but society still stigmatizes mental illnesses. GAD sufferers often need encouragement from family members to seek medical care.

I know that fear and anxiety will always be a big part of my life. I can't handle it alone, but with the support network of my friends and family, I'm learning to cope with my disorder. When I get too fearful, they remind me to take one day, one hour, one minute at a time. And even I can deal with one minute.

Examining the Persuasion in "Generalized Anxiety Disorder (GAD), A Real Illness"

Clearly, Linda Kulp is trained by experience and treatment in the difficulties and management of Generalized Anxiety Disorder, a type of anxiety she defines for us with accounts of her behavior and situation. She uses that knowledge to discuss (via description and narration) scenarios readers empthasize with even if they haven't expcricnced life exactly the same way. She convinces us to help GAD sufferers and perhaps anyone else with anxiety by taking their problems seriously and being supportive in particular ways. Her experience before diagnosis and with her husband even after diagnosis contrasts to her experience with a new friend and with her sons. Because Kulp itemizes the help others can offer those who suffer this anxiety, readers finish the essay feeling enabled. Reading Kulp's list, following her vivid account of her panic in traffic, her husband's lack of attention to her problem, and then his "booting" her out of the house makes us feel that being supportive is the least we can do! Her narrative approach to revealing the symptoms of her anxiety, discussing the way she avoided counseling at first, and finally, illustrating the success she has today persuades readers that they can help people they know who suffer anxiety simply by showing them this essay.

You can analyze the essay in terms of how it utilizes the five ingredients of the argument and persuasion essay:

The assertion: GAD is a real anxiety condition and people can help those who suffer this kind of anxiety.

At least three supports: The author describes her anxiety, the medical diagnosis, the conditions that made it worse, its genetic component, and she itemizes actions and behaviors that are helpful to the sufferer.

The crescendo: The argument opens with a vivid description of anxiety behavior before the diagnosis and the response of the speaker's husband and friends. It takes readers on a worsening journey, portraying the detrimental behaviors of the spearker's husband. Ultimately, as the speaker takes charge and gets a diagnosis, her marital relationship is still strained. Finally, after a divorce, therapy, gaining new friends and supports and including her son in the situation, the speaker is well informed about the conditon and what kinds of help sufferers need.

The opposition is dealt with early as the speaker recounts the reaction of those around her who could not understand her anxiety as a medical condition. The opposition point of view is even represented in the speaker's reluctance to enter counseling.

Images and details that speak directly: The argument is made with details like horns wailing behind the speaker when she can't make the turn, with the list of questions she asks herself in her anxious state, with the making of the turn when actually there is not enough room. Reported speech gives attitudes directly. Facts offer the feeling that the speaker is in the know on her topic.

In another argument and persuasion essay, Christi Killien argues that people who adopt "hurt" children need more support and community resources than they might realize. She portrays her own experience with adoption and its outcome for the adopted child and his siblings along with facts and information she has garnered from six years of work in adoption services. She attempts to persuade prospective adoptive parents to recognize the need for services to deal with difficult outcomes.

Adoption Not Always the Stuff of Fairy Tales

It was the middle of a blazing Houston summer in 1970 when my parents decided to adopt a 3-year-old boy. They were both 37 years old and already had three children, two girls and a boy. I was the oldest, an adolescent with long blonde hair, skirts I rolled up short on the way to school and a pile of *Glamour* magazines in my room.

Dad told us we would meet our new brother on a get-to-know-you outing at the Houston zoo. Fine, I remember thinking, but will it take all afternoon? We stared as Tony scraped every crumb of his McDonald's hamburger off the table into his mouth. Later, my parents explained how Tony had been abandoned by his alcohol- and drug-addicted birth mother, along with his three younger brothers, one of whom died of malnutrition.

This, in 1970, was no reason to assume that Tony had been affected. At least not by anything that a good family couldn't heal in a jiffy. My parents could create a better present so that the past no longer mattered.

Mom told me recently that the minute Tony came into our house, she felt the tension. When Tony stole and lied, as most kids do, Dad wouldn't leave him alone. Dad was enraged that Tony wouldn't admit it or even cry. I was astonished that he wouldn't cry. I was crying all the time, when I wasn't arguing his defense. My brother David coped silently, but neither of us could seem to connect to Tony or enjoy him, either.

My sister Leslie, who is much closer to Tony in age than David and I, clearly did connect. Leslie and Tony were comrades. She truly loved him. I say loved, because he is dead. Tony had just turned 19 and was in the Navy when on April 4, 1986, he hanged himself on his ship. For months afterward, I'd wake up in the night gasping for air, grieving for Tony, for myself, for my failure.

Working at the Northwest Adoption Exchange for six years, I learned that many of the families who adopt special-needs children (this means anyone but healthy infants) and do it well, especially in the black community, are associated with a church. It is an act of faith, no doubt about that. My dad was a very religious man. But for us, religion, like good intentions and even love, wasn't a match for the challenges of raising a very hurt child.

Without the support of a community and specialists, our family crumbled under the weight of it. At work, I thought about Tony as I wrote little biographies of the kids that went into our royal blue binders and onto our Web page. If Tony were in the system today, I'd no doubt be obliged to include in his profile the usual litany of diagnoses: Attention Deficit Hyperactivity Disorder, Reactive Attachment Disorder, Fetal Alcohol Effect and Post Traumatic Stress Disorder. There would be medications and therapy, or at least, awareness.

I thought about my parents when I learned that kids who have experienced extreme neglect and abuse often can't attach normally. Adoptive parents of these children get frustrated and angry at the pervasive detachment; in fact, the adoptive mothers, who take the brunt of the child's unconscious fear and anger, describe the sensation as being attacked.

In addition, kids with the kinds of neurological disorders that Tony must have had don't learn cause and effect. Logic and natural consequences are so many vapors in the room. Tony wasn't capable of blending in or of following the rules. His early brain formation and lack of nurture sabotaged his life. But that isn't the only information I've needed to understand what happened.

What I also learned is that my mother and dad could never have parented him. They had no support, and they had misplaced reasons for adopting Tony in the first place. A sense of benevolence, of needing to share, is not enough. You have to understand the individual child's terms, adjust expectations for attachment and achievement, reach out to every one and any one who can help and then pray. That way, when you realize that you're in over your head, chances are much better that the story won't end in tragedy for you or for your adopted child.

Examining the Persuasion in
"Adoptions Not Always the Stuff of Fairy Tales"

Christi Killien writes for those who think adoption is a solution to problems or is a benevolent thing to do. She urges them to look again when it comes to special-needs children and to take into account some hard facts— that goodwill and religious fervor can not address the difficulties such children bring with them. Evidence that communities with a very strong support system for families experience success, means all families adopting "hurt children" must find similar support. The increased tension and anger in Christi's home when her adopted brother came to live there and his suicide at age 19 are very persuasive that this course is not an easy one. When she retroactively applies the technical information she learned from working in the adoption field to her home situation, Killien's clarification of things makes the situation even more disturbing. That only one factor makes a difference adds to the urgency in this article. Find that support, Killien says, or you will drown in the consequences of adopting a "hurt" child.

Here is a break down to put things in terms of the necessary ingredients of the argument essay:

The assertion: Adopting hurt children puts a strain on families and on adopted children that can prove lethal and perhaps only one condition helps the situation: participation in a supportive religious community.

The three supports: Although the parents believed that there was no reason to assume Tony was deeply and permanently affected by his early environments and that adopted parents can create a better present so the past no longer matters, Christi's mom admitted that she felt tension as soon as Tony came into the household. Christi's behavior as well as that of her siblings changed. Tony ultimately committed suicide. Researchers know that the consequences of early detrimental environments often include neurological and psychological disorders.

The crescendo: We witness the speaker's first meeting with Tony, we learn about Tony's difficulties with Christi's dad and his suicide, and we learn about the speaker's subsequent job experience in the adoption field.

The opposition: A paragraph is devoted to the community the speaker found out does well in this area.

Images and details that speak directly: The little boy Tony eating every crumb of his McDonald's hamburger, his inability to cry when his adopted father yelled at him, the speaker waking up at night gasping for air, the list of diagnoses associated with hurt children, the sensation of adoptive mothers feeling attacked, the description of impaired children's behaviors, and the misplaced reasons for adopting.

A Short Sermon to Help Give You Confidence with the Argument and Persuasion Style

In an essay entitled, "The Distance Between A Hero and A Human Being," columnist Ellen Goodman argues that we in the United States need to understand what a hero is. When she wrote her essay, papers had just been published verifying Martin Luther King's extramarital affairs and graduate school plagiarism. She believed that Martin Luther King should continue to be admired for his leadership despite the revelations. In her argument essay, she quotes Clayborn Carson, the head of the King-paper project, "I don't think it's healthy in a democracy to believe that there are some people who were born great and not without human flaws and limitations." She quotes King himself in a sermon, "I want you to know this morning that I am a sinner like all of God's children, but I want to be a good man, and I want to hear a voice saying to me one day, 'I take you in and I bless you because you tried.'" Herein lies Goodman's assertion: It is valuable for Americans to use this new information about King's adultery and plagiarism not just for a revisionist view of King, but for a revisionist definition of what constitutes a hero. We must change, she says, from thinking heroes are saint-like versions of people, versions we create and can never ourselves match. We must begin to see that heroes are human beings, flaws and all, who serve humanity by finding greatness within themselves when the times demand it.

We can find the greatness inside ourselves when we are called to. That call sometimes comes in the form of a deep desire to write what we have witnessed or lived through in order to persuade others to take steps or adopt thinking that leads toward the improved health of our community.

Exercises and Tips for Gathering Your Material

Your experience has informed you. It may have taught you to do some things differently from the way you used to or the way other people do it. It has taught you to change the way you think. Here is a procedure to help you get at material about what you have learned and answer the "write" question for the argument and persuasion style essay.

Conducting a Survey

Divide a sheet of paper into three columns. Label one column "personal experience," one "social experience," and the last, "educational/vocational experience." Jot down any and all experiences that come to you under these headings. Your columns might look like one student's sample on the next page.

Some experiences I think of as vocational are in the column headed social, such as hotel management. My student's experience of hotel management must have been more social than vocational when she made this inventory. That is fine. You do not have to have the experiences in the right column, so much as use the columns to brainstorm and list the extraordinary number of experiences you have had.

Personal	Educational/Vocational	Social
Dating	Going to college	Being part of the local arts community
Being single	Trying grad school	Growing up middle class
Family Council	Learning dance	Being part of a neighborhood
Only daughter/adopted	Social work	Hotel Management
Youngest	Writing Courses	Fundraising
Being in debt		Event Planning
Youngest child		Festival Production
Breaking up		Waitressing
Renting apartments		Recruiting and Training
Being a friend		Personnel
Deciding on college		
Deciding career		
Being childless		
Living miles from family		
Losing friends		
Making new friends		
Dabbling with Tarot		

After you make your lists using columns, ask yourself which items in the columns generate passion for you right now.

Making Assertions

Once you have selected what I call "passion items," which are the items on your list that you feel are important to informing your experience, write some assertions about them. For instance, a passion for me is talking about how to raise children after divorce. I assert, "A divorce can be the opportunity for parents to enrich their children's emotional development." As soon as I write this assertion, I hear a chorus of voices disagreeing or getting upset or saying, "How can you say that?"

"Good!" I say to myself and the chorus of voices. "I have something to convince you of! I know what my work is."

According to my assertion, I have to show you how divorce can offer the divorced parents an opportunity to raise emotionally enriched children.

Using Assertions as Building Plans for the Essay

Unlike writing the other essay styles,, in argument and persuasion essays, you know your insight ahead of time. Assertions are required in writing argument and persuasion essays. They help you write them and act as building plans.

According to my building plans, I can support my assertion by using several styles of essay writing. I can narrate anecdotes from the lives of my own children. I can distinguish the characteristics necessary for good emotional development and show how they are present in the divorce. I can contrast my experience raising children in one two-parent household with my experience raising them in my single-parent household while sharing them with their dad's household to show increased opportunities for my children's emotional growth.

Stay out of the Fog

Assertions are always statements, never incomplete sentences, never questions. I could not write a strong argument if I merely wrote, "Raising children when you divorce." I could not write a strong argument if I merely asked, "Can a divorce be the opportunity for raising emotionally enriched children?" My answer to that question is yes, but the word "yes" is not a plan—it doesn't tell me cause and effect or define emotional enrichment. The answer to that question in a full sentence is an assertion. My assertion keeps me focused on what I am going to say to back it up and on the order that will best help me support it. The assertion is not only a plan; it is a lighthouse guiding me away from the rocks of illogic and incoherence.

Write the assertions you can think of concerning your passion items. Select the assertion that most interests you. There are two more exercises ahead before you start writing.

Supporting the Assertion

Your personal experience may include the following information to support your assertion, or you might seek some of this information as you are writing:

- the testimony of experts, authorities, and others who should know
- statistics
- comparisons of essential nature (an essay I read compared all of us who use up the planet's resources to airplane mechanics who pop rivets off a plane and say there are plenty more to keep the plane together)
- the history of how something happened
- the effects of something that happened
- solutions to a problem
- an account of the opposition's argument (the chorus of voices I spoke about earlier) and way of thinking
- your counter to that point of view.

By reporting opposing points of view, you show your astuteness and your respect for differences of opinion. This invites readers to consider your opinion. Providing the opposition's point of view credits you; it shows you have looked deeply into your situation.

To start developing your essay, write your assertion across the top of a blank page. Then list the supports and evidences you might use in making your argument.

This process may have some surprises for you. Sometimes you'll make an assertion you feel strongly about, but when you begin to support it, you'll find you have more ammunition for the opposite side. Well, switch sides then!

Organizing the Argument and Persuasion Essay toward Crescendo

Now that you have written your assertion and thought up supports for it, decide on the order you will use to present the supports for a powerful argument. A good strategy is to put your strongest support first and tuck in the weakest next. Then you can put your third strongest in and after that your second strongest. This will help you get the reader's attention and keep it. You don't want to let your argument wind down or fizzle out by exhausting your best arguments first.

Develop a Draft

Linda Kulp starts her essay at the changing of the stoplights when she was unable to put her foot on the gas pedal. Christi Killien begins hers with the blazing heat of a Houston summer. Both openings capture the emotional heat behind their author's argument. Where can you start your essay to place yourself in the experience that led you to want to persuade others to think or behave differently?

The famous journalist H.L. Mencken began an essay in support of capital punishment by providing a summary of the opposition's point of view: "Of the arguments against capital punishment that issue from uplifters, two are commonly heard most often . . ." After stating the two in one sentence each, Mencken writes, "The first of these arguments, it seems to me, is plainly too weak to need serious refutation." He spends a short paragraph refuting the first argument. He spends the rest of his essay refuting the second argument, which he believes has more force but contains fundamental errors.

Keep Drafting

Look at the order of the arguments in both Kulp's and Killien's essays. Think about the emotional strength of the arguments and the way the order of the arguments keeps you reading and considering the authors' points. Look for the places where each author considers, addresses, and defeats opposition. When you receive responses to your draft, think about whether the response indicates that the order you are using to make your point works as strongly as it can. Think about the ways in which you address those who would oppose your point of view. Are you answering a significant argument they make? Do the facts and anecdotes you use help people consider your point in spite of opposition to it? You don't have to take on every single point that an opponent might make. You do need to identify what you believe to be the most important opposition views and why you believe that. You need to formulate ideas that defeat the opposition.

Notice that Killien addresses the opposition with her story about her family experience, which bursts the bubble that good intentions equal success. By focusing on one community that does better than most with the adoption of special needs children and mentioning the reasons they do have better outcomes, Killien demonstrates that she has studied the opposition. Having done so, she is in a position to argue that if you don't have this kind of community support, you will have much difficulty. Kulp addresses her opposition with anecdotes about people who responded to her anxiety by dismissing it. This is the opposition she is trying to enlighten with facts and information about what people can do to help those who suffer with GAD.

After you develop your argument based on your first round of response, get additional response. Then you might want to leave this piece alone for several days. When you come back to it, are you still persuaded? Does this writing represent what you believe? Can you see the importance of what you have lived now that you have written it in this style?

Chapter XI

Prepare the Fruit for Market

We continue to seek more good literary or cultural essays. Send only your best work.

> —Editors, Boulevard,
> *Triannual Literary Magazine*
> 2001 Writer's Market

Now that you have essays that are shapely, you want them to sparkle. It is time to use the editor inside, or an editor that you hire, to ready your work for publication—whether that means sending out to a magazine or handing your writing around to family and friends.

I believe that you can almost always do much of the editing yourself for style, accessibility, grammar and punctuation if you know a few rules.

In fact, the editor in most of us so strongly wants to fulfill every English teacher's expectations that we are lucky if we got to write freely while drafting without the urge to edit before enough of our experience was on the page.

Hopefully, as you wrote your essays, the playful and sculpting parts of your writing self were at work, and that red pencil schoolhouse marm had a well-deserved vacation. Now welcome the detail-oriented eagle-eyed teacher in you back to enthusiastically (and perhaps even cheerfully) dot your i's and cross your t's! With your essays fully formed and making good contact with others emotionally, it really does become more fun to work on surface issues and polish them up.

Here are my quick tips to improve the appearance of your essays and impress those who read your work:

Spelling and Frequently Confused Words

Never let a document leave your computer without using a spell-checking program; however, that is no substitute for your own careful read. Look very carefully for sound-alike words that you may have used improperly. Spell checkers won't pick up that you have used *they're* for *there* or *our* for *hour*. You can easily write the word *write* when you mean *right*. And of course there are the typos that spell check will not find—i.e. missing the ending "n" in "then."

Review contractions; know when to add the apostrophe and when not to. You add the apostrophe when you mean it is, you are, they are, etc. You do not add the apostrophe when you mean possession as in *its* hair, *your* hair, and *their* hair.

Be alert for frequently confused words like accept and except. Accept means to receive something willingly. Except means but or excluding.

Affect and effect are two other frequently confused words. Affect is a verb that means to influence, and effect is usually a noun, which means a result or an impact. You can affect a person's feelings and then have an effect on that person.

There are many more frequently confused words, of course. *The Least You Should Know About English* by Teresa Ferster Glazier contains a good list of them with explanations.

Capitalization

A common question about capitalization is when to capitalize directions. When we are naming regions of a country, the South, the Northeast, for example, we capitalize the words but when we are giving compass directions, we do not: "Turn south as the intersection and then east at the stoplight."

Special names are capitalized. This includes places, titles, and people. Penelope, Vice-President of Internal Affairs, spoke on the phone from the West Coast. Common names are not. "She talked to us about the subjects one must take to get a good foundation for a good future in the field of finance: calculus, statistics, and accounting."

Although a title with a name is always capitalized—President Lincoln and Governor Smith—a descriptive phrase offering occupational or ranking information does not require capital letters: "Jeffrey Kensington, a doctor."

Father, mother, grandmother, and other familial forms of address are capitalized when they appear without pronouns. "I love you, Grandmother, and I will stay to help you." When they appear after a pronoun, they are not capitalized: your father, her mother, and my grandmother, for example.

Words in titles are capitalized unless they are articles, preposition, or conjunctions that do not come at the beginning of the title. "To Live or to Die, " "For Ever and a Day," and "Take a Clue from the Kitchen" are three examples where interior articles, prepositions, or conjunctions are not capitalized.

Paragraphing

After frequently confused words and capitalization rules, paragraphing often causes the most lingering questions. Magazines and newspapers have allowed paragraphs to grow shorter and shorter, leaving them only one sentence long at times. I believe in well-balanced paragraphs that a reader can settle into. A one-sentence paragraph is a jarring event that should be experienced only sparingly. When you are writing, notice how your thought patterns continue and vary and stray and come together. Make your paragraphs indicate these patterns. On a computer, it is easy to play with paragraphs, joining sentences into big blocks and then breaking the big blocks up if they seem overwhelming. Your finished product should have a nice look about it. That is subjective, but the eye can help. Just as we like sculpture to have curves and bulges and sleek areas, we also enjoy this on the page before us.

Pay attention to transitions. Paragraphs should flow one to another, whether through images, phrase repetitions, time phrases, or spatial indications. When you get response to your drafts, your readers will let you know if your transitions lose or jar them. Ask people their opinion if you are unsure that you have kept them with you as you move to a new paragraph.

You may have learned that all paragraphs must have a topic sentence, two to three middle sentences and a concluding sentence, or something like that. This kind of write-by-the-rules method is too confining for today's essayist, but the idea that a paragraph has enough in it for the reader to settle into is important. Remember, literary personal essays expand experience by making readers (and the writer) pay attention to information that might not usually have the spotlight. For paragraphs to help the essay do its work, they must not all be the same length and most of them must be longer than the one sentence paragraphs we commonly find now in newspapers and magazine.

Who and whom — The Rules

You will often find "who" used today in places where traditional grammarians would say "whom" is necessary. Language changes according to the way people speak, and even the rules for written language change if people consistently veer from certain constructions. In the case of "who" and "whom," the traditional approach is this: use who if the word introduces an independent clause: "Who will go to the movies with me?" Use "whom" if the word is the object of a preposition: "To whom will I give the price?" The non-traditional approach goes like this: If your words sound stuffy because you use "whom" go ahead and use "who." For instance, "Who did you give it to?" might sound right to you.

Is it bad to end your sentence with a preposition? Not really, we do it all the time now. We say and write sentences like, "Where is it that I am going to?" and "Where did you get that delicious dessert from?"

How Do I Know Which Form of Each Pronoun to Use?

I, he, she, you, they, we, and it all work as subjects, the agents performing the action. Me, him, her, you, them, us and it all work as the receivers of the action: "She gave them and me a gift." "She and I gave him and you a gift."

When Do I Use Hyphens between Words?

Use hyphens if words join together as adjectives describing a noun: "three-year-old Jason James" or "top-notch students"; also use hyphens if the words become a noun: "stick-in-the mud" or "hole-in-the-wall" or "three-year-old." "More or less" is a phrase that doesn't become a noun; hence no hyphens. Certainly, use hyphens when a word would definitely mean something else without a hyphen. For example, there is a great difference between resign and re-sign in the case of a ball player. The use of hyphens in other words or upon other occasions is tricky. Some word combos you believe are adjectives, like much loved, do not require hyphens. If you are in doubt, dictionaries can help, but even most editors looking to accept your work will not know these rules themselves and will ultimately rely on copyeditors. Also consider the context. In this book, for example, I have not used hyphens in the names of essay styles because I thought the words looked cumbersome with the hyphens and because the first edition of this book also did not hyphenate these terms.

Do We Spell out Numbers or Use Arabic Numerals?

The rule of thumb used to be that non-technical writing required that numbers be written out and that two-word numbers have hyphens. Technical writing called for writing out numbers below ten and using numerals for those numbers above ten, unless the number started the sentence off. In my work as an editor, even in non-technical writing, I now use numerals for numbers over ten that do not start a sentence, but some writers always use Arabic numbers.

What Are the Tricks to Using Punctuation Correctly?

Concentrate on in the rules about punctuating quotes and dialog, and learn where commas go and do not go in complex sentences.

Whatever someone says is in double quotes, "Like this." The punctuation at the end of the sentence usually goes inside the quote marks. If the speaker is also quoting someone else, the quotation marks around the words the speaker is quoting are single quote marks: "That's what the man said to me. He said, 'Turn right and then left.'" Notice that there is a comma before the quoted dialog.

Dialog broken up by an insertion should be set off with commas. "That's," Jamie screamed, "what the man said to me. He said, 'Turn right then turn left.'"

By the way, when you write lines of dialog, each time a new speaker speaks, start a new paragraph.

When quoting others' words verbatim, use quotes if they take up three lines of type or fewer in your document. If they require four or more lines put a colon after your last word and then indent the quoted lines but do not put quote marks around them.

Commas go after introductory clauses or phrases: *When the moon rises,* some dogs like to howl. *After my bedtime,* the moon rises.

Commas go before and, or, but, yet, and nor in compound sentences, except when the first independent clause is very short: *The river is high and the currents are strong,* but he wanted to raft down its waters despite the high risk.

Commas set off nonessential information that describes someone or something. Nonessential means that readers would know the subject or object even without the extra information because the subject or object is a proper noun: Charlton Heston, *a well-known actor,* announced he has Alzheimer's disease.

If readers wouldn't know which group or person or thing the writer is designating without the modifying information, don't use the commas: "The group who had never written an essay reported to room 101 while the group that had experience writing essays reported to room 102."

Commas divide items in a list. Using a comma before the "and" that joins the last item to the list is optional now. Many people feel that using it makes their sentences more clear. Others feel that the extra comma litters the sentence. You can write, "For his camping trip, Jason James, an equipment enthusiast, packed his tent, sleeping bag, flashlight, water bottles, freeze-dried food, a change of clothes and a floating flashlight," with or without the comma after clothes. The publisher of this book likes the final comma. It is a style decision. When one of your items is a compound item, like bread and butter, you might want to use that last comma for clarity: "I served coffee, fruit cocktail, scrambled eggs, toast and butter, and orange juice."

Use semicolons when one related independent clause ends and another begins and you are not going to make them into two sentences: "No matter when she and I get together, we always start our conversation the same way; we always talk about our hair."

Always use a semicolon before however, therefore, and moreover if they start an independent clause: "I want to go to college; however,

I can't afford the tuition." Notice that the "however," which is introductory in its independent clause, is followed by a comma. You can also always make this kind of construction into two sentences: "I want to go to college. However, I can't afford the tuition."

What are Dangling and Misplaced Modifiers?

It is really easy in English to create phrases that are meant to modify a subject and then forget to put the subject in, leaving the modifier describing something ridiculous: "Running around the neighborhood, a fire flamed in the garbage can" should be written as "Running around the neighborhood, I saw flames in a garbage can." It wasn't the fire that was running. "At sixteen, my father gave me the keys to our family car" should be, "When I was sixteen, my father gave me the keys to our family car" because your father was not sixteen when he gave you the keys. In your final reading of your work, ask yourself whether your phrases describe the action of the being or object they were meant to describe. "While answering the doorbell, the water in the pot of simmering vegetables boiled away and the vegetables burned," is not okay. "A purse was found by the detective weighing about twenty pounds" doesn't work unless the detective is a leprechaun.

What Is Passive Construction and Why Should I Be Careful about Overusing It?

Nothing slows an essay up like passive construction. Passive construction makes reading an essay feel like you have started down a familiar road only to find you must navigate around orange traffic cones and reduce your speed. We use passive construction either because we think it sounds more formal or because we are self-consciously aware that we are imagining something and writing about it. "The event was attended by the company's staff" would be much better stated this way: "The company staff attended the event."

Having a clear subject in your sentence makes everything more immediate for the reader. "At the event, the tables were decorated with three-foot wide buckets of flowers" goes down easier and is more dramatic this way: "Three-foot wide buckets of flowers decorated each table."

What Are Non-Essential Words and Phrases?

Never bulk up the writing just to hear the sound of your voice going on longer. I once worked with a woman who said "literally" and "in my mind" so much that I never paid attention to what she said. There are few occasions when you will have to remind people that you are speaking literally or even call their attention to the fact that you are using figurative language. "I believe," "in my mind," "truly" and "very unique" are among the often-used phrases that clutter writing up and call unnecessary attention to the teller of the event. In the case of "very unique," the adverb qualifying the adjective negates the meaning of the adjective—to be unique is to be one-of-a-kind, in essence, not by degree. Our speech is filled with meaningless phrases. Keep them out of your writing unless you have a good reason to use them (when communicating the flavor of a person you are describing requires that you repeat a tag line they use again and again, for instance).

Modern writing aims to be assessable and to sound like normal everyday speech. Sometimes we think that "folksy" phrasing makes our essays accessible and speech-like. Usually, instead of helping the tone, though, these phrases hinder it and make our writing harder to understand. Delete phrases like, "I, myself," "that's another story," "in order to," and "in a sense." In addition, be careful about using the word "would." Why make things conditional when you can avoid that uncertainty? For instance, the sentence, "Following my recommendations will help you create manuscripts that editors enjoy reading," is stronger than, "If you would follow my recommendations, editors would enjoy reading your manuscripts."

Although sometimes it is okay, the abbreviation "etc." finds its way into writing too frequently. If you can think of three examples of what you are listing, write them rather than using "etc." You sound more astute and less lazy that way. If you can't think of several examples, are you sure your readers will be able to?

What is Subject-Verb Agreement?

This is important! Don't use a singular subject with a plural verb, or vice versa. Pay attention to the agent in your sentence and to the agent's action. In the sentence, "Each of the writers has a notebook," *each* is singular so I use the verb has. "Some of the writers have notebooks" has the plural subject, *some*, therefore, the sentence uses the verb have, which agrees in number with a plural subject.

- Words like dozen, crowd, family, and class are singular.
- Both, all, and most are plural.
- Everybody, one, and no one are singular.

What Are Noun-Pronoun Referents?

When you use a pronoun, it must have a clear noun to refer to. It replaces that noun in its part of the sentence. "I've always liked comedy and have decided to train to become one" uses the pronoun one to mean comedian but since the noun that one refers to isn't in the first part of the sentence, the pronoun has no clear referent. The sentence can be fixed to read, "I've always liked comedy and have decided to train to become a comedian," or "I've always like comedians and have decided to train to become one." Although the meaning of sentences without clear pronoun referents may still be clear, it is much smoother to read sentences when the referent is clear.

One of the most confusing pronoun problems in our language today involves gender. Our convention used to be a default "he." "Whenever someone wants to make a call, *he* can pull a cell phone from his pocket" sounds funny today. Some grammarians have decided that the plural but genderless "they" can replace the gender-identified pronoun, even when a singular pronoun is called for: "Whenever someone wants to make a call, *they* can pull a cell phone from their pocket." This grates on my ears because they and their are plural and someone is singular. I reword my sentences to avoid this problem: "Whenever people want to make calls, they can pull their cell phones from their pockets." If I absolutely do not want to change from the singular, I usually say she instead of he. This is because I am a woman writing; I might expect a man writing to choose he unless he thought his audience was primarily female.

When you set about polishing the spelling, punctuation, paragraphing, sentence grammar and capitalization in your essays, try to have fun. You will usually find a few good laughs:

I want to eat my baby brother, yelled the words and rushing to the cupboard the box of raisins fell on the floor.

Chapter XII

Trucking the Fruit to Market

There are many different routes a writer can follow to get published, but no matter which route you choose, the end is always the same—becoming a published writer.

—*2004 Writer's Market Guide*,
Writer's Digest Books

W hen you think about publishing your essays, consider that there are several kinds of markets: literary and small press publications, national and international large circulation publications, local newspapers, regional and national newspapers, radio, industry publications, and online sites and publications. It is rare for a writer to start at the top with national and international publications before publishing locally and regionally. In working to get your writing published, you will benefit from understanding market categories, the publications' openness to new writers, and submission requirements and protocol.

Many published directories help you learn more about markets and submission protocols. Perhaps the most widely known directory is the annual *Writer's Market* from Writer's Digest Books, usually available at library reference desks. It includes information on the submission process, notes from editors about what they are looking for and over 8,000 periodical and book markets. Another good reference is *The American Directory of Writer's Guidelines: A Compilation of Information for Freelancers*. Now in its third edition from Quill Driver Books, this directory lists over 1,000 periodical publishers and 400 book publishers as well as information on the submission process. *The International Directory of Little Magazines & Small Presses* from Dustbooks lists over 4,000 markets in the small press niche.

All of these directories list addresses and editor names to use when sending in work, but you should check online or by phone to see if the editors' names are still current as people change jobs frequently. The directories also indicate whether publications require authors to query first about editors' interest in seeing their work or if they can send unsolicited essays for consideration. Generally, the smaller the publication, the more likely they are to read unsolicited manuscripts, but sometimes the smaller magazines have particular reading periods and will not accept work for consideration outside of designated months. The directories will include information on these reading periods.

Market Categories

When you are submitting in the nonfiction category, you might especially look at market directory listings for literary magazines, women's and men's magazines, news magazines, trade journals, regional interest magazines, and specialty topic magazines (such as those devoted to guitar playing, yoga, or hiking). Think about the interests your essays address. Find listings for publications that address audiences with the same interests.

In addition to searching for publications in market directories, check the manuscripts wanted section of the publication *Poets and Writers, Magazine,* available at newsstands and in libraries. Many editors collect contributions for themed anthologies by advertising in this magazine's "manuscripts wanted" section where they describe the books they are creating and the kind of material they want. Usually it is fine for the essays to have already appeared in periodical literature, but not in book form.

Another category for publication involves contests. Professional writers' organizations, arts commissions, and educational organizations and institutions as well as particular presses and publications sponsor contests for essay writers. Often they list the essay category as nonfiction or creative nonfiction. Most of these contests are listed in *The Writer's Market* and in *Poets and Writers*. An entry fee of up to $25 dollars per essay is not unusual to support the advertised prize money. Often, entrants receive copies of the winning work, a year's subscription, or back issues of a publication in addition to having their work considered for the contest. If you believe a contest's sponsoring agency is reputable and you believe your essay (or essays) is as finished as you can make it, entering contests is a reasonable way of participating in the publishing community. Should you win, your work will appear in a juried publication. In some cases, this leads to book publication. Sometimes, book publishers have agreed to publish the book-length winners. In other cases, arts commission sponsors award grant money for winning writers to hire a press to publish the work. These books are often also up for awards by regional consortiums. Sometimes acquisition editors read winning essays in magazines that sponsor contests and contact the winning authors about book-length manuscripts. And, of course, it is always a plus to be able to write in your bio or cover letters that you are an award-winning author and to name the prize and the contest judge who selected your work (usually an established writer in the genre).

As you read listings of interest in directories, magazines, or newsletters from arts organizations, keep a file with notes on the publications' and editors' names, addresses, and phone numbers.

Include whether the editors are open to reviewing unsolicited manuscripts (meaning manuscripts they did not seek directly from a particular author) or require a query before they'll tell an author whether they want to see work. Note whether the publication offers guidelines online or by mail and if to receive them, you must send them an SASE (self-addressed stamped envelope). You will not regret keeping all of this information in a computer file or notebook or on index cards. The information adds up and you don't quite know when you will be using it. Having it handy in an organized file will pay off by saving you time when you are ready to submit work.

Guidelines

In addition to sending for submission guidelines, as part of your market search, go online and type the name of the magazines you have found in the directory into your search engine. Often magazines post their guidelines on their web sites, where you can download them. The guidelines give you information about preferred word lengths, topics, and deadlines. They tell you whether the editors will consider multiple submissions. This is the term for the practice of sending work to several publications simultaneously. Since some publications take a long time to respond to writers (the guidelines will usually give you some idea of the normal wait time for response), writers often send work out to several places at a time if the publications say they consider work that is also being considered elsewhere. Usually these publications require you to let them know should any other publication take the piece while they are still considering it. This way, if the magazine requires first publication rights or if the magazine that has taken the work requires all rights, other editors can stop considering the piece. Making note of the rights the magazine requires upon publication lets you avoid mix-ups and keep editors happy. In addition, with good research, you can send your essays to non-competing publications and broaden your potential audience.

Guidelines often talk about when payment is made (upon publication or upon acceptance). Sometimes they stipulate the amount of payment.

Some guidelines offer specifics about the format editors prefer for manuscripts. These specifics may include details like where you put your name, address, phone number, and email address and how much space to leave between lines. Most of the time, publishers prefer double spacing and names on the top right hand corner, along with a word count. They like sheets with numbered pages rather than bound copies. Guidelines specify whether the publication allows or encourages email queries and submissions. If they do, they will indicate the email address and word processing format they desire for the submissions. The guidelines also tell you whether the editors want a brief bio along with your submission.

Knowing the guidelines is essential in placing your essay. If you cannot find the magazines' guidelines online, mail an SASE to receive a print copy. If the magazine is overseas, include an International Reply Coupon (IRC), which you can purchase at the post office, instead of standard U.S. postage.

The Submission Package

Imagining the editors' side of the desk will help you when you are preparing your submission packages. Editors have deadlines by which they have to review submissions, and they have more manuscripts sent to them than they can possibly publish. They have more to do than choose writing, and they have mountains of paper to keep track of. They need contact information at their fingertips because they are always pressed for time. Sometimes, junior editors and other editorial staff pre-read submissions and bring them to the attention of the editor. Because submissions are handled by many people and put in many inboxes, pages can get separated from one another very easily.

When you submit your manuscript, check each set of guidelines to make sure that:

- your name, address, and telephone number appear exactly where the guidelines ask for them to appear, whether that is on the cover letter only, on the first page only, or on all the pages
- you fasten the pages as requested (often editors don't like staples)
- you meet posted deadlines (usually a postmark on the deadline date is sufficient)
- you send your submission to the correct editor or editorial department, using the exact names you find in the most current listing or guidelines

Incorrect names or names of editors no longer working at a publication delay the arrival of your submission on the right desk. Many editors find it disagreeable to deal with submissions from people who haven't kept up with the very magazine in which they want to publish their work.

Rarely will editors call you to tell you they have rejected your piece; most often they won't call even to say they have accepted the piece. The US mail (or email if they accept submissions that way) works best for them. Again, include an SASE with any written correspondence.

Feel comfortable contacting the publication about your work if you haven't heard from the editors in the promised amount of time. Be prepared for a variety of answers: We are behind and will be finishing our process soon; we have no record of your submission (please re-send it or never mind, it is too late to resend it); we have decided not to use your essay but haven't yet sent rejection letters; we are waiting to make a final decisions while we hear from those we have already accepted.

Query Letter, by Mail or Email

Larger-circulation publications with limited room for essays and articles by non-staff writers often require a query. To make sure of this and to learn whether you can query by email, read the guidelines. Take any statement that editors require a query letter seriously.

If you can't find the information you need in the guidelines, you may have to call the editor's office. Most likely an assistant will answer and give you the information you require and the name of the editor to whom you should address your materials.

If you do need to send a query letter first, and it has to be mailed rather than emailed, write it in standard business format on white, 20-lb. paper and enclose it in a #10 white business envelope. You may attach one or two short samples of your published work, and if they do not fit well folded with the letter, use an 8½ by 11 manila envelop.

Your query letter should be around one page in length. You want to be brief, but if it takes a bit of the next page to state your case, take the space to introduce yourself and your work and explain why you believe the editor would be interested in considering your essay. The query letter is akin to the cover letter I discuss in the following section, and most of the requirements are the same. However, because the essay is not included with the query letter, you have to work a bit to interest the editor in wanting to see it. Therefore, in your letter, tie your essay to something topical or illustrate how it is on target for the particular magazine you are querying. If your essay is about a regional or national celebration or is well suited to national observances such as Black History Month or Memorial Day, let the editor know the essay will fit a particular issue of the magazine. Because such issues are planned way in advance, you must often submit topical essays a year or so before you think publishers will want to print them.

In a query letter, you want to catch the editor's attention and focus it on your essay. Sometimes asking a question works: "What do people from middle America think on Memorial Day?" or "How do parents of young children explain Martin Luther King Day?" for example. The answer to your question presents a reason why the editor might want to print your essay. Next, describe your essay succinctly telling what readers will get from reading it (here's where you can tie in the topical spin). Give some background on yourself that reveals the reason you would have an original viewpoint concerning your topic.

Here is an example of the body of a query letter written two different ways for a personal essay that includes some historical information. Look at the cover letter in the next section for more ideas on focusing an editor's interest:

Why do adults often need to revisit family secrets long after they seem to matter? My personal essay is based on the benefit I received from investigating a court case against my father that my parents hid from me. In the essay, I recount the way I was drawn to a box of papers in the basement of my childhood house but knew I shouldn't open the box and what happened when after the death of my mother, I did open it. I believe the experience I had in discovering more about my father opened up many talents I'd long ignored.

Many of us baby boomers are interested in revisiting family secrets as a path to self-growth. This essay is especially appropriate in an issue of your magazine devoted to life review, since it focuses on how previously guarded aspects of one's life affect later years.

Over the last five years, I have published many essays in local newspapers and literary magazines, including the *Greenwood Dispatch and Sunflower.* I am a frequent speaker for conferences on family histories and parenting. I am hopeful that you will invite me to send my essay manuscript, "Boxed Secrets Imprison Talent" for your consideration for publication in the "Speak Out" section of *Growing Older* Magazine.

Or:

How does government secrecy born of mistakes during turbulent times affect future generations? My personal essay recounts the uncovering of my father's post WWII court case, lost because the government claimed that documents needed for evidence contained secret information. My mother had kept the results of the case from me after my father died, but years later as a middle-aged adult, I researched the story and interviewed people who had shared my father's experience. My essay reveals much about case and the effect of government secrecy on family life and personal development.

I believe the point of view and historical information in my essay are a fit for *Vets View Magazine,* devoted to the ongoing stories of those who serve in the military.

Over the last five years, I have published essays in local newspapers and veterans' organization newsletters, including the *Greenwood Dispatch and Peninsula News.* I am a frequent speaker for Veteran's Day programs, and I am hopeful that you will invite me to send my essay for your consideration.

Cover Letter Accompanying the Submission by Mail or Email

Most literary publications do not require a query letter. For these editors, you include your essay in your submission along with a cover letter. Their guidelines will inform you about the topics and word lengths of the essays they consider.

Think of your cover letter as your chance to interest the editor in your work and introduce yourself. It has to be succinct and to the point. You do not want to wear editors out before they read the essays you submit.

Even if you submit by email, the effective cover letter is written as a formal business letter. You send it to a particular person with a particular position at a particular publication. Unless the editor is a Dr., you can use the first and last name as the salutation without a Mr., Mrs., or Ms. Again, you can check by telephone to make sure the information you retrieved on line or in a directory is correct. The inside address includes your name, address, telephone number, fax if you have one, and email address.

As for query letters, print letters should be typed rather than handwritten on white 20 lb. paper and placed in a white #10 business envelope. Single-space your paragraphs and double-space between the paragraphs. A simple font is best. Editors may judge a fancy font and fancy stationery as all show with no substance. Your writing should convey your strength as a writer, not your paper.

In the first paragraph, introduce yourself and your essay. Tell what you are submitting and why you are submitting it. Include something you notice about the publication you are submitting to. For example:

> Born and raised in New York City, I have spent my vacation time the last five summers as a farm hand at my uncle's ranch in Wyoming. Because of my experiences on the ranch, I have been writing about the ways that working with animals has influenced my political outlook. I am submitting one of my essays entitled "Round Up" for your consideration for the "Now I Speak" section of your magazine. I believe readers will relate to and enjoy the "city girl has a hard time learning the ropes" aspect of my experience. Moreover, they will be encouraged to take a sobering look at the way the lack of open space and large animals on their horizons shapes their opinions, policies and ideas. In reading your magazine, the range of American experiences offered in each of your issues impresses me, and I believe my essay will certainly add to that range.

In the second paragraph, fill the editor in on any background that introduces you as a writer and qualifies you to write on the topic:

> My work has previously appeared in Midwestern and East Coast literary publications such as *Spinning Wheel* and *Under the Earth.* One of my essays won first prize in the 1996 New York State Arts Commission sponsored writing contest judged by Jim Julien and has since been anthologized in *Writers Write on Green Pastures.*

End your letter formally by stating that you look forward to hearing from the editor:

> I have enclosed an SASE for your response and look forward to hearing from you.

> Sincerely,

Reread your letter to make sure there are no misspellings, typos, or grammatical or paragraphing errors. Then fold it in thirds with the addressee's name, title, and address facing up and slip it into a business-size envelope. Address and stamp the SASE, fold it in thirds, and put it in the envelope with your letter. Fold your neatly typed, correctly spelled, double spaced, dark-enough-to-read essay pages as one and insert them into the envelope. If the essay is too long to fold neatly into the #10 business envelope, use an 8½ by 11 envelope instead. You can paperclip your SASE to the essay in this case.

Before you mail the essay and cover letter off, note in a submission log when, based on the guidelines, you expect to hear from the editor. If you haven't heard by then, allow one more week and then check by phone or by email to see if the editor has received and considered your submission.

The Bio

If the publication guidelines ask you to include a short bio, write three to five sentences describing yourself and your writing. Bios are most often written in the third person: "Eliot Elderberry is a poet and boat builder." Some authors write about where they live and work and with whom they live: "Currently, he lives in Mendocino with his wife and two cats." Some use the space to list publications they are proud of or positions they hold: "He has published in several wood-working magazines as well as in his town's weekly newspaper and sits on the local school board." To get a good idea of what a bio looks like, read them in copies of the magazine you are submitting to. They are usually called "Contributor's Notes"in the publications. Model your bio after the ones you admire, including honest things about yourself that you feel comfortable having the public read, should the essay be accepted. Include the facts that relate to the essay you are submitting: "Eliot Elderberry has written extensively on financing public education in small coastal towns."

Again, if you are sending hard copy, include an SASE for receiving the acceptance or rejection letter. It used to be that the essay would also be returned. This is often no longer true, as postage is more expensive than copying and printing; besides, once a submission has been read by many people, it shows.You probably should send a fresh copy each time you submit your essay and state that there is no need to return the hard copy.

Some believe that if you have already sent in an SASE with the query and the editor has asked to see your essay, you do not need to send another SASE. I think it can't hurt to make the editor's life as easy as possible. Perhaps she'll accept the essay but want to send it back to you with some suggested changes. Perhaps she's lost the original SASE or used it to notify you that she is interested in seeing the work.

Handing Rejection

In this business, rejections are more frequent than acceptances. And due to the numbers of submissions editors are handling, most rejections are form rejections rather than personal letters. Editors seldom offer advice, comments, or reasons for the rejections beyond the catch-all phrase, "Your work did not fulfill our needs at this time."

How do writers cope with impersonal rejection? Some writers collect the form letters and use them as evidence that they are engaged in the profession. Keeping the rejections is also a good way to maintain your submissions log. If a particular editor has rejected your work three times, you may as well stop submitting work to that editor and cultivate a new one. If you happen to be lucky enough to get some handwritten comment at the bottom or in the margins of a rejection form letter, those notes can provide you a fresh look at your work, the way you approach editors, or the appropriateness of your writing for the magazines you targeted.

If you feel that your work is ready for publication despite a rejection, figure out additional publications you can submit the work to, type out new cover letters, and make your new submissions. On the other hand, waiting for an essay that has gone out into the world to return to your desk provides time and distance from the work that can help you better understand what a rejecting editor thought needed fixing (even if they haven't written comments). You might want to rewrite before you submit the work again.

When you make submissions and deal with rejection, you are participating in the publication process. You grow as a writer each time you participate in this process. Even if you work is rejected, you learn more about submitting while you gain the confidence and record-keeping skills necessary to make successful submissions in the future. Most importantly, you have made the work of submitting part of your writing life.

Building Professional Relationships with Editors

One day, you'll receive a letter of interest from an editor or a note scrawled on a rejection form saying the editor would like to see other samples of your work. Do not delay in getting back to the editor. Get back quickly,while the editor remembers who you are and why your work interested her. I suggest email or sending hard copy of other writing with a letter explaining why, based on what the editor said, you believe your new submission might suit her publication. As with your earlier submission, do not be too quick to follow up with a phone call, but if a month goes by, a call or an email is in order to find out if the work is being considered.

If the interested editor subsequently rejects the additional work you sent and later that work is accepted for publication elsewhere, write to let the editor know. Say something like:

> I was delighted by your interest in my work and although my essay, "Another Day, Another Way" was not quite what you were looking for, based on your interest I submitted the essay to *Wrangling World*. It will appear in the March issue. I am at work now on more essays and hope to submit one or two for your consideration in the near future.

Although they are very busy, editors are human. They enjoy hearing that they have made a difference in the lives of writers, even if they were unable to publish them.

Never, however, call or write an editor and beg her to publish your work or tell her how to create a better publication. Reserve those suggestions for a letter to "from our readers."

The Contract

When that great day arrives and a publication accepts one of your essays, you will receive a contract. In some cases, this contract may be the acceptance letter telling you that you will receive a free copy of the issue you are in as payment for your work. It may state that the publication reserves the right to publish your work in an online issue. Because more and more publications have gone online, you should definitely ask about this possibility. If you don't want your work on the web, you need to tell the editors at the time you receive an acceptance letter. Typically, smaller magazines "buy" first publication rights, freeing you to re-publish the essay in other places. Should you allow your essay to be placed online? Having the piece accessible on the web may or may not interfere with future publication. Some magazines are not interested in material that is available elsewhere. On the other hand, an editor for an anthology may see it and select it.

If the publication pays in dollars as opposed to copies, you will receive a contract that spells out what the publisher is buying. It can be first publication rights, first rights for a certain amount of time, which keeps you from re-publishing in other magazines for 90 days or so, or all rights. This is usually so the publisher can anthologize or resell the work without your permission, although they must always acknowledge you as author and tell where the work first appeared. If the publication is a quality one and you want to appear in it, you may well say "okay" to the all-rights terms. If you are unsure about the publication, you may not want to give them such global rights. The same goes for electronic rights. Ask the editors if you can amend the contract to read that they are reserving first publication rights only and that after the article appears, control of the rights reverts to you. Perhaps they'll accept this offer. If they refuse and you don't want to agree to the contract, say "thank you for your consideration" and tell them that you will be submitting the work to other venues.

As for the amount of money you'll be paid, there may be room for negotiation if the price has not been set up front. If the guidelines give a per-word, per-page, or per-essay amount you have little or no wiggle room. If the publication hasn't advertised any rate of pay and makes an offer, than you can ask for more. Choose a percentage more that you feel comfortable requesting—ten, twenty, or thirty percent more. How much more you'll get may depend on the size of the publishing house. The Chicken Soup for the Soul franchise may have more money behind it than a smaller trade publication. Certain trades have more money to invest in publishing than others—magazines about writing, for example, pay much less than magazines about computing. Glossy national magazines have bigger budgets than tabloid newsletters.

Publishers will reject your requests, meet them, or suggest compromises. Again, you must weigh your desire to make money against your desire to see yourself in print and build a portfolio of published essays.

To get that contract may require spending as much, if not more, time pursuing publication as writing. You'll enjoy yourself as you do this if you view the research as aiding your writing as well as your publication effort. To familiarize yourself with the publications on the always-growing list of those seeking manuscripts, make frequent visits to the periodical rooms of libraries and to newsstands and bookstores. Really browse the offerings. You will notice many magazines that are new to you. Look through them, and you will become acquainted with markets you hadn't known existed at the same time as you realize you have more topics to write about than you might have believed. If a magazine strikes you as a possibility, either go to the library and look at back issues or order some from the publisher. You may be able to find some archived issues and portions of current issues online. Get a good feel for what the editors publish. Write down the submission information, which usually appears on the first inside page along with subscription information or in the "about us" or "how to submit" section of the online version.

In addition to reading publishing guides and familiarizing yourself with publications that take essays, ask any publishing author you know about the who, how, when, where, what, and what next of their publishing experience. Their answers will be extremely informative. You will see how they follow the rules and how they bend them.

Getting into the swing of things by submitting your work is just like writing—something you have to start on your own and something you ask for response to while developing your process.

When the work of finding markets for your essays seems to drain your writing time and writing energy, stop and read some essays that have been published (I have some suggested places to find them in Appendix II). Notice how important you felt it was to read the essay and how much you enjoyed being in the author's presence. Make peace with the idea that you will spend time bringing your essays to the attention of others. Think about how the time you spend will prove worthwhile when many, many others read your essays and benefit from your words.

An Example of the Three-Step Response Method

*M*arjorie Ford sent me an essay-in-progress that she was having trouble completing to her satisfaction, and I helped her develop the work using my three-step response method. After I read Marjorie's undeveloped draft, I wrote to her, dividing my response into the three steps of Velcro words, Feelings, and Curiosity.

Fire

Each morning since fire ravaged our mountain community, turning generations of trees to stark black sticks and our cabin to a bed of ashes, I wake to the same words: It's all gone.

As I lie in bed, powerlessness covers me like a scratchy old blanket. My own mortality cackles from the closet. Meaninglessness chills my bones. Old losses storm against the window. Anger and helplessness battle for air.

Each morning, "It's all gone," grief's tenacious voice drones.

And each morning, I move on and out into the world, putting the voice aside, inside. I attend to people or to writing, to nature or to learning, the things I live to do. Then, suddenly, in the middle of anything, my mind uncovers another treasure in the ashes. Gone.

The quilt. Heavy, but not too heavy to cuddle under while reading. Sometimes for an entire snowy day.

My mother's rocker. Padded by the mostly pink pillow she stitched together in a crazy quilt pattern from baby clothes we had sewed for Michelle.

Jeff's third grade painting. A waif of a boy gripping the tail of a huge white bird lifting them both from an emerald green mountain into a bright blue sky. After all these years, the colors remain as true as I remember Jeff himself.

Needlework by Mom. Thick yellow and orange yarn depicting Michelle's grade school painting of the sun. It smiled down on Michelle and Jeff as they slide down a rainbow in their red wagon.

A client's charcoal drawing. Given to me by her husband after she died. A woman's face, as serene as still water, just like her face, and then again, not like her face at all.

Frank's gift to me. It was the birthday after my own cancer returned. A simple line drawing of two hands holding each other above a poem about walking together on beaches and in forests and in heaven after death.

"It's just stuff," I scold myself, but my untamed-first-thought-morning-mind persists. It is more. Weeks later I look through photographs, one taken during five-year-old Ellie's first sleep-over alone with us on the mountain. A perfect picture had made me reach for my camera.

I had gathered a basketfull of moments to remember that weekend.

Hiking oh-so-slowly down the hill to the village, we stopped to examine every rock and flower reflecting color in the clear, mountain light.

Playing Pooh Sticks in the tiny stream at the base of the hill, just like Christopher Robin and Pooh would do if they were here.

Discovering dandelion balls waiting just for us to send off their shimmering fluff with our secret wishes and dreams.

Plastering a cake with Blue and Red and Green and Yellow patches of frosting. Like a crazy quilt covering the cake and Ellie's mouth.

Eating PB and J sandwiches, the bread cut with a heart-shaped cookie cutter. To entice Ellie to eat something more than frosting for lunch.

The exchange—of words and more—between us when I tell her the noise that startles her is Tata cleaning out the fireplace. "I love your Tata so much," I add. She tilts her head to the side then flashes her big blueberry eyes. "Nani, I think you love everybody!" I think to reassure her that I don't love everybody the way I love her. But her confident face says, "Let it be." It's okay, I think, to remember your grandmother loving a lot of people.

Each experience imprints in my mind, but the one my camera will record is of Ellie at the huge second-story window. She kneels motionless, entranced by the clear Arizona sky and dense pine forest, like an innocent at mass. Silently, slowly I soak in her wonder. Breathlessly I raise the camera. The window frames Ellie's back and the trees, mountain ridge, and sky.

When I snap the picture, the camera whirs. Ellie turns, but not immediately. Her mouth is set in earnest concentration, her eyes dart among ideas. She is pondering a big question.

"Nani," her words step gently, "Is this a tree house?"

I think to say, "No," bound by truth. But I confirm the creation her eyes and ears have pieced together. "Yes. . . it sort of is," I tell her. Because that is the larger truth.

As I look at the photograph, I long to know the larger truth about the fire. About loss.

The next morning, "It's all gone," does not greet my waking. Instead music booms between my ears, over and over again.

"Shower the people you love with love. Shower the people you love with love." A cliché out of nowhere.

"Shower the people you love with love." A cornball jiggle jangling over and over.

"Shower the people you love with love." Annoying me as I shower. And dress.

"Shower the people you love with love." God, stop it!

"Shower the people you love with love."Harassing me all through my day. Until I get it: Memories of love are what survive—because they are the larger truth.

My Response to This Draft

Whether I am reading an essay or listening, I respond to what I hear. I read it aloud to myself and think about the essay in the three steps I have dubbed Velcro words, Feelings (with subcategories of feelings in the service of the essay and feelings that distract), and Curiosity. This response is intended to help writers develop their drafts. Editing for paragraphing, grammar, and punctuation is not part of the Three-Step Response Method, and is best considered after the drafts are developed. Even so, editing happens naturally during the Three-Step Response Method. For example, as Ford's essay developed, sentence fragments became complete sentences. She also combined and lengthened paragraphs as she worked from the feedback I offered.

Here are my responses to what I "heard" while reading Marjorie's draft:

Step One: Velcro Words (The Words and Phrases That Stick with Me upon First Hearing)

fire ravaged community, cabin to a bed of ashes, it's all gone, quilt, rocker, third-grade painting, needle work, a woman's face serene as water, cancer returned, in heaven after death, just stuff, examine every rock and flower, Pooh Sticks, shimmering fluff, crazy quilt covering the cake and Ellie's mouth, bread cut with a heart-shaped cookie cutter, more than frosting for lunch, Tata is cleaning out the fireplace, you love everybody, innocent at mass, is this a tree house, larger truth, about the fire, about loss, shower the people you love with love.

Step Two: Feelings

A. Overall Feeling I Have in Response to Reading the Essay

I feel the sadness of losing a life's worth of mementos; I feel the speaker's love for her granddaughter as well as the relief and surprise of being able to replace feelings of helplessness and loss with positive feelings of love.

B. Feelings That Divert My Attention

After the statement, "It's just stuff," I find myself wondering where the speaker is writing from. It doesn't seem possible that she is in the home that burned, yet she doesn't talk about being displaced.

The essay seems to center on a particular event—Ellie on her first sleepover. The speaker tells us that the experience has imprinted itself on her mind, though she recorded only her one moment at the huge second-story window, entranced by the clear sky and pine forest. Later, when the author says, "I had gathered a basketful of moments to remember," I am confused. I thought she only chose one moment to record. Does she mean she took lots of pictures and the basket was filled with them or is the basketful a metaphor? Additionally, at this point in the essay, it seems to me that the speaker would be aware that she doesn't need anything tangible to remind her of happy times. On the other hand, it was the picture that reminded her of this. As a reader, I have been given a conundrum that takes me away from the speaker's insight.

I don't immediately understand how saying, "Yes, the house is a tree house" speaks a larger truth.

I am confused about why the photo of Ellie at the window survived.

I feel told that the repeated line about showering those you love with love is annoying, but don't feel annoyed.

I am surprised that the speaker considers the "larger truth" of the fire.

I feel uncertain about the very last line—"Memories of love are what survive—because they are the larger truth." Instead of reading as if this were truly discovered by the speaker, it reads as if the speaker wants to believe in them. I am forced here to accept a larger truth without experiencing the speaker's coming to a new epiphany about the loss of the household of memories.

A small thing: I am distracted by wondering whether Tata is a person or an imaginary friend.

Step Three: Curiosity (Where I Am Curious to Know More)

Where is the speaker writing from? Does she find that memories of both love and not-love survive? How do memories survive if the tangible objects that fostered the memories are now gone? What must the speaker do to preserve memories when reminders are missing? Showering people with love creates memories of love, but is that why the speaker takes the action of showering them with love? The speaker says she chose one Ellie moment to record with a camera; how does she feel now about that choice? When the morning phrase shifts is the speaker surprised? What does she feel at the change? Why is the new phrase annoying? Is it from an actual song she knows?

❧

After she received my responses, Marjorie mulled over what she considered the "conundrum" I had uncovered with my questions about Ellie and the memories of good times with her centering on one photo. She agreed that she didn't like the explanation in the last line either.

In the days she spent thinking about her essay, Marjorie often felt like giving up on the essay. But one morning, she awoke from a disturbing dream and while writing it down, had an "aha" experience about the ending to the essay. She re-titled the essay, "What Survives" because, as she said, "What survives is what we have right now to show people we love them. Paradoxically, 'now' doesn't just survive, it thrives at some point. The now message in what I sent you is the one consistent with the gift cancer brought me. I'd wondered how I lost it in the fire. Clearly (now that I see it) the lyric brought me back to that quite blissful, lively way of being."

Here is the revision Marjorie sent after mulling and her "aha" experience:

What Survives?

Since forest fire ravaged our cool mountain getaway, turning generations of trees to stark black sticks and our cabin to a bed of ashes, I wake each morning with the same thought: It's all gone!

I lie in bed, despair weighing me down like a rough, heavy blanket. Questions chill my bones. Why? Why me? Do I deserve this? Anger battles helplessness for air. Old losses—to disease, divorce, death—storm against the window. Mortality cackles from the corner.

Each morning, the same message greets me. It's all gone!

And each morning, I move on and out into the world, putting the grim voice aside, inside. I attend to people or to writing, to nature or to learning, the things I live to do. Then, suddenly, in the middle of it all, my mind uncovers another treasure lost in the ashes.

Mama's maple rocker and the mostly pink pillow she stitched in a crazy quilt pattern from scraps of Michelle's baby clothes. I could smell a hint of Mama in those objects. They held only the good of her.

My stepson's third grade painting. A tiny boy grips the tail of a huge white bird lifting them both from an emerald green mountain into a bright blue sky. Through the years, the colors remained as true as I remember Jeff himself.

Mama's embroidered translation of Michelle's second grade painting. Thick yellow and orange yarn recreated the sun shining on Michelle and Jeff as they slid down a rainbow in their red wagon. Michelle, like I, thought Jeff and his father would be a family with us forever.

A client's charcoal drawing of a woman's face, as serene as still water, just like her face, and then again, not like her face at all. Her husband gave it to me after she died.

Frank's gift to me on our anniversary after my own cancer returned. A line drawing of two hands held each other above a poem about walking together in forests, on beaches, and in heaven after death.

And perhaps hardest of all: A particular photograph of Ellie, my five-year-old granddaughter.

It was her first sleep-over with Nani and Tata on the mountain. When I saw her gazing out of the second-story window, kneeling like an innocent at mass, I reached for my camera. Silently, holding my breath, I raised it to my eye. The lens framed the window framing her back, and beyond her, the dense pine forest, the high mountain ridge, and clear Arizona sky. It captured every sensation of the weekend.

We had meandered down the hill to the village, stopping to examine each rock and flower, like dogs sniffing their way along a path. Colors reflected in sweet mountain light while we played Pooh Sticks in the stream at the base of the hill, like Christopher Robin and his playmates. Dandelion balls posed along the road, waiting for us to send their fluff shimmering off with secret wishes and dreams. Ellie couldn't know that my wish was for more years than doctors predicted, enough time to build solid memories of me that would live on in her.

We had baked a chocolate cake and she plastered it with blue and red and green and yellow patches of frosting, like a crazy quilt covering the cake and her mouth. I enticed her to eat more than frosting for lunch with PB and J sandwiches made with a heart-shaped cookie cutter.

A sudden thud startled her until I told her it was Frank cleaning out the fireplace. "I love your Tata so much," I added. She tilted her head to the side, then flashed her big blueberry eyes. "Nani, I think you love everybody!"

I thought to reassure her—"I don't love everybody the way I love you"—and to defend myself—"I'm not a fool"—but her confident face said, "Let it be." It's okay, I decided, if she remembers me loving a lot of people.

When I snapped the picture of Ellie gazing out the cabin window, the camera whirred. She turned, but not immediately. Her mouth was set in earnest concentration, her eyes darted among ideas. She was pondering a big question.

"Nani," her words stepped gently. "Is this a tree house?" I thought to say, "No," bound by truth. But I confirmed what her eyes and ears had pieced together. "Yes. . . it sort of is," I told her. Because her creation was the larger truth.

The photo of Ellie enchanted at the window held the whole weekend—especially my faith that we would play together at the cabin in the future.

Now my heart begs, "Does nothing last?"

Quit being maudlin, I scold myself. It's just stuff. But my untamed-first-thought-morning-mind knows better. They were treasure tucked full of good times, sensations, relationships, hope. Now they are gone.

Then one morning instead of being greeted by the grim message I had come to expect, I wake with a familiar lyric singing itself in my head. As outrageous as a river raging through a roaring fire, it echoes over and over, "Shower the people you love with love."

What?

"Shower the people you love with love." The mocking sentiment inserts itself like a clown at a funeral.

"Shower the people you love with love." As I bathe and dress, it repeats like a broken record. I can't turn off that old James Taylor lyric: "Shower the people you love with love."

The words harass me all through the day. They won't leave me alone—until in a flash as if by magic, the dots connect, and I get it—the larger truth. The "it" I "get" is the resurrection of cancer's greatest gift, the one I lost in the fire.

Temporarily.

The persistent truth is this: We have now to show people we love them. I can do that still, before they are lost to time, divorce, death (theirs or mine).

We always, only, have Now. Now is the gift that comes tucked inside the jolt of loss. Now survives to use as we choose.

My Response to the Revision

I read this version with most of my curiosities satisfied and a delight in the feelings I was living through Marjorie. At the end, though, I did have a feeling response that brought me out of the essay:

Step One: Velcro Words

"the good of her," and "clown at a funeral," and "the dots connect," among others.

Step Two: Feelings

A. Overall Feeling I Have in Response to Reading the Essay

I definitely feel both the poignancy of losing the memorabilia, the love for the grand-daughter, and the author's attentiveness to her and to the world and to joy despite, or because of, cancer and fire's devastation. I am aware that the image of the quilt and lying under it on snowy days is gone, but I didn't miss it. Perhaps, I was drawn to the images that connect the speaker with people and the remembered liveliness of the times at her mountain home. I know that the earlier repetition of the word "quilt" in "crazy quilt pattern" didn't really build emotion. But in this draft, emotion builds early with the questions, "Why? Why me? Do I deserve this?" By raising these questions, the author introduces other losses, and her agitated state becomes palpable. I am interested to learn that Michelle's second grade painting was done during happy blended family years and that the ending of that family was one of the speaker's previous losses.

B. Feelings That Divert My Attention

Feelings that left me with a letdown this time came with the new ending. First, a "persistent" truth is not the same as a "larger truth," so I didn't feel the writer had used her earlier thinking to inform the ending. I also felt as if the speaker had summarized her change rather than letting me experience it with her. I wanted to see the speaker living by her new insight. I wished to see definite action.

Step Three: Curiosity

I know from the start that it is a second home that has burned to the ground. I know that the objects uncovered are definitely those of memory sprouting here and there during the days that followed the loss of the house.

I understand why the objects that are lost matter to this particular essay—they are reminders of what is gone but not gone. The memories are still there, and ultimately the speaker arrives at something more intangible than memory: the NOW.

I no longer feel confused about the photograph of Ellie and the situation it was taken in. I notice that the "basketful" is gone now. I know what the author means by the larger truth concerning the tree house and ultimately concerning life.

I now know the phrase she repeats about showering others with love is a familiar one, and with the new analogies, she convinces me that she is annoyed when it repeated again and again while she is mourning the fire's destruction of her home and what it meant to her.

The phrasing this time clears up my confusion about who Tata is. The speaker states that the sleepover is with Nani and Tata, and she lets me know she told Ellie that Frank was cleaning out the fireplace. Then, she includes the direct speech, "I love your Tata so much." This clears up my curiosity about who Tata is, although I didn't know *Nani* and *Tata* are Spanish for grandma and grandpa until Marjorie told me. Even so, reading those words in the context of this version of the essay didn't take me out of the essay.

After receiving my new responses, Marjorie eventually sent the essay back with a new ending, one that provides much more than a summary. However, this new ending didn't come, she said, until, "I gave up trying."

When an essay is important to us, it brews in our unconscious. Portions of it pop into consciousness and dreams when we aren't looking if we have been working hard on the writing. In *The Courage to Create*, Rollo May discusses the way "aha" experiences often come after we have transitioned from work to relaxation or from relaxation back to work. When we put away a piece of writing we have slaved over and pursue other activities, solutions to our writing problems do often present themselves.

Here's the ending that came to Marjorie. In the essay, it goes right after the words, " . . . and I get it—the larger truth."

> The "it" I "get" is a resurrected cancer-gift, the one tucked inside the jolt of mortality. A treasure I lost in the fire. Temporarily. The inescapable truth is this: I always, only, have Now to show people I love them.

So now I cuddle and smooch and play with Ellie like a half-grown puppy. And when I hold her in my gaze, my heart beats faster. With others, too, I say, "I love you," whenever it fits. It pops out of me like flesh escaping the top of a girdle. I don't care if I sound foolish, inelegant, indiscriminate. I know I am not. And when people I haven't seen in years appear in my mind, I search for them on Internet directories: a long ago therapist who helped me turn my life around; the junior high school English teacher who modeled confident womanhood and told me I could write; the boy, long since a man, I thought I'd grow up to marry; the graduate school professor who shaped my thinking about all things being connected. We email, we talk on the phone, we meet each other if we can.

I let them know what they mean to me, while Now burns hot and bright.

This time around my responses were as follows:

The action with Ellie and the long list of people who occur to the speaker is very satisfying at the end because it takes readers into the new "now" and gains momentum for this way of being in the world. We actually experience the energy of unleashing love and gratitude. The truth is again the "larger" truth, so it is in line with her thoughts earlier in the essay that arose from the notion of a tree house.

Note: In the completed draft, although there are some fragments used stylistically, having to put more down on the page encouraged this author to use full sentences instead of fragments and to use more variety in paragraph lengths. Some editing happens as a consequence of reacting to response, even when the writer isn't concentrating on editing. The step of editing is most effectively used after the writer has used the three-step response method to fully develop the work. Chapter XI (page 179) contains tips and information on this final step in writing essays.

As always, when I share the three-step response method with writers, I feel a deep sense of satisfaction at how this method provides what authors need to fully communicate both to themselves and others, even when they have been frustrated with their material and their abilities to "get it said" on the page. In this case, Marjorie Ford dug deeper and deeper into what the lost objects and memories meant. In doing so, she changed fire from a great destroyer to an illuminator and releaser of life energy.

Appendix II

A Cornucopia of Resources

I hope this book has helped you formulate and answer many important questions about how to write personal essays and get started publishing them. The essay world is big and more and more resources become available daily. Here is more information you might find helpful.

Books on How to Write Essays and Find Subjects from Your Experience

The Situation and the Story by Vivian Gornick strives to answer the essayist's question, "How does one pull from one's own boring, agitated self the reliable narrator who will tell the story that needs to be told?" Using memoirs and essays of the past hundred years, the author traces the changing idea of self, demonstrates the truth speaker in essays, and teaches how to hear the truth in our own and others' essays.

Tell It Slant: Writing and Shaping Creative Non-Fiction by Brenda Miller and Suzanne Paola offers descriptions and samples of "varietal" personal essays and digs into another form, the lyric essay, quite extensively. Miller's and Paola's accompanying Website, www.mhhe.com/tellitslant, has useful essay samples, publishing information, and exercises.

The Art of Creative Non-Fiction: Writing and Selling the Literature of Reality by Lee Guttkind contains a true insider's knowledge on choosing topics, the nuts-and-bolts of technique, the intricacies of marketing, and the ethical and legal issues of "truth."

Write From Life: Turning Your Personal Experiences Into Compelling Stories by essayist, fiction writer, and poet, Meg Files, teaches writers how to transform their raw experiences into finished pieces so they can identify story-worthy material, conquer fears associated with personal exposure, determine a story's focus, and shape the material into a cohesive whole, then edit and revise as needed.

Write Your Heart Out by Rebecca McClanahan is a mixture of direct instruction, writing exercises and prompts, examples from published and unpublished texts, and personal reflections on the writing process. Through explorations of journal writing, memoir, writing about joy and sorrow, letter writing, and collaborative writing, McClanahan encourages those who want to write.

Unsent Letters by Lauren B. Smith offers help to those who want to use letter writing as a tool to attain the peace that comes from resolving issues of conflict, love, worry, and devotion. Although the book is not about writing for publication, writing unsent letters can help writers free themselves up to approach difficult but important work that leads to essays.

Becoming Whole by Linda Joy Myers, PhD is a guide to writing life stories to transform trauma into healing, mastery and wisdom. Myers' chapters include thoughtful exercises and writing samples. In addition, the book contains helpful information about organizing memoir and using techniques of fiction.

The Writer's and Teacher's Collaborative in New York State (www.twc.org), 5 Union Square West, New York, NY 10003-3306, 888-BOOKS-TW, Telephone 212-691-6590) maintains a catalog of useful books for the essay writer.

Writing About Your Life: A Journey into the Past by William Zinsser contains 13 chapters in which the author and acclaimed teacher takes you along on his journey through years of writing, editing, teaching, and traveling. To provide an instructional model, he explains the technical decisions he made as he wrote the essays

Books and Web Resources for Help with Grammar and Style

From Strunk and White's famous *Elements of Style* to thesauri to MLA style guides by every major publisher of college texts, there is so much out there on editing that you could spend all your writing time sorting out resources and information. Althyough you don't need to become a professional copyeditor to get your work accepted, you do need to write prose that adheres to spelling, punctuation, capitalization, and phrasing style conventions and that reads smoothly and well. Here are a few of my favorite sources on editing because of their accessibility and the simplicity with which they impart information:

Grammatically Correct: The Writer's Essential Guide to Punctuation, Spelling, Style, Usage and Grammar by Anne Stillman, Writers Digest Books. This is an excellent resource, especially for information on spelling and frequently misused words.

The Least You Should Know About English Writing Skills by Teresa Ferster Glazier, Harcourt Brace Jovanovich College Publishers, in many editions (Form A Fifth Edition is my favorite in the series). Glazier includes everything you every really needed to know about English spelling and grammar but your teachers made too complicated to figure out. Even so, it is a slender volume, not like those fat texts and workbooks you remember.

"Avoid Common Grammar Pitfalls," by Becky Ohlsen, *Writer's Digest* Magazine, August 2002. A professional copy editor distills the process of editing for "tight, lean prose devoid of errors with 22 tips" phrased so that you can use and remember them.

Plumb Design's visual online thesaurus at http://www. plumbdesign.com/thesaurus/index.html is fun to use, and you will realize that unless you are repeating a word for emotional impact, there are many words that are precise for your specific meaning and by using them, you sound informed and insightful.

http://www.thesaurus.com has a load of grammar tips. This site is worth browsing from time to time to sharpen your self-editing skills. You will find pearls of practical wisdom that will inform your writing.

http://www.mhhe.com/socscience/english/links/writelinks.html includes links to dictionaries, thesauri, grammar guides, writing sites, language sites, and more. Jack Lynch's Guide to Grammar and Style at the link to http://www.andromeda.rutgers.edu/~jlynch/ Writing/ is very easy to use.

http://intranet.cps.k12.il.us/Standards/Programs _ of_Study/ pos_ High _School_ Programs_ of_St/ pos_ High_ School__ Language_ Arts/ pos_ English_ III_ Programs_of_St /poslag_ 03_ websites.pdf is part of the extensive Gutenberg project, which is attempting to connect many studies of the English language. The links on this page include ones to a grammar site, a site about speeches and how to document them, and a Modern Language Association (MLA) style guide site good for those using research in their essays.

Magazines for Help in Writing Essays

Writing It Real is my online magazine for people who write from personal experience. I offer my instruction weekly in articles that include writing exercises, accounts of subscribers' revision processes, and information on publishing, among many other topics. *Writing It Real* is geared to helping writers start, develop, and polish essays and poems as well as understand the writing community. Visit www.writingitreal.com for subscription information and to read sample articles.

Poets and Writers is a bi-monthly publication well known for its articles about authors, presses, and publishing as well as for each issues' information on writing programs, workshops, contests and manuscripts wanted.

Joining the Associated Writing Programs (see the degree-program listings below) and receiving their magazine, *The AWP Chronicle,* is also a good way to regularly read in-depth articles by writers who teach.

The Writer offers writing advice from famous authors as does *Writer's Digest.*

The smaller press publication *ByLine* presents articles on the craft or business of writing, including regular columns on writing poetry, fiction, nonfiction and children's literature and publishes short stories and poetry, with a special feature for student writers.

Directories for Publishing Information

For Manuscripts Wanted

Writer's Digest's *Writer's Market* offers up-to-date comprehensive lists of magazines and publishers seeking manuscripts. There is an online version available as well. See your bookstore or library for this directory or order it directly form the publisher.

Writer's Guidelines: A Compilation of Information for Freelancers from More than 1,400 Magazine Editors and Book Publishers, Quill Driver Books is easy to read and use for locating markets for essays and articles.

The *International Directory of Little Magazines & Small Presses* from Dustbooks lists over 4,000 markets in the small press niche.

Again, *Poets and Writers* has a well-known and well- used manuscripts-wanted section. Reading the "seeking submissions" listings helps you find editors to send your work to, because many of them advertise there for specific theme anthologies.

The Writer and *Writer's Digest* include market listings in each issue. *ByLine* sponsors contests.

Magazines for Libraries offers writers an additional way to research publications. It is available at library reference desks. The magazine includes information on the editorial slant and financial backing of hundreds of publications. Reading this guide can help you decide if and how your essays match a specific magazine's mission. Reading it can also help you discover more topic areas for your writing.

Online Markets for Writers: How to Make Money by Selling Your Writing on the Internet, by Anthony Tedesco and Paul Tedesco, offers a thorough description of the on-line market and explains its background and development.

Guerilla Marketing for Writers by Jay Conrad Levinson, Rick Frishman, and Michael Larsen, also from Writer's Digest Books, offers many tips essay writers can use. Chapter 12, "Weapons Made Possible by Your Ability to Write," is of particular interest as it concerns op-ed essays and book reviews.

Finding Agents

Writer's Digest's *The Writer's Market* includes listings of agents and literary agencies.

The Writer's Guide to Book Editors, Publishers, and Literary Agents, Prima Publishing, is another useful resource.

Visit http://www.aar-online.org for useful information from The Association of Author's Representatives.

For Writer's Conferences

Writer's Digest at www.Writer'sDigest.com and *Shaw Guides* at www.shawguides.com jointly offer up-to-date listings on conferences worldwide.

Particular issues of *The Writer, Poets and Writers,* and *Writer's Digest* also offer annual listings. You might check back issues at the library or in online archives for many of them.

The *AWP Official Guide to Writing Programs* includes some information about writers' conferences. For the guide, contact the Associated Writing Programs at George Mason University in Virginia: The Associated Writing Programs, Mail Stop 1E3, George Mason University, Fairfax, VA 22030, (703) 993-4301, awp@gmu.edu.

Degree Programs

The AWP Official Guide to Writing Programs has information on 300 programs in the US, Canada and United Kingdom as well as on 200 writers' conferences, colonies, and centers. Its preface helps you understand how to choose the program that fits your dreams. The nation's undergraduate and graduate writing programs belong to the association. For a complete listing of graduate and undergraduate writing programs, contact the Associated Writing Programs at George Mason University in Virginia: The Associated Writing Programs, Mail Stop 1E3, George Mason University, Fairfax, VA 22030, (703) 993-4301, awp@gmu.edu. The organization's publication, The *AWP Chronicle,* is filled with useful articles by writers who teach in the various programs as well as information about the programs, including popular low-residency programs for professionals who want to earn MFAs while living and working a distance from the schools. These programs offer long distance mentorship and regularly scheduled program meetings.

Extension, Continuing Education and Online Courses

For these programs, call your nearest university, college, and community college, as well as any state university and community college extension campuses and ask whether these campuses offer classes or certificate programs in creative writing, magazine writing, memoir, or creative nonfiction. Programs such as those at the University of Washington in Seattle, the University of California Los Angeles, the University of California Berkeley, and Pima Community College in Tucson all employ distinguished writers in their programs and put out brochures and bulletins.

If you live in an area that is not rich in schools, the local arts commission may help you locate a program through their listings and literature.

If you prefer working from home with others or a writing tutor, visit www.absolutewrite.com and www.writers.com. You will find many courses taught by popular writers whose names you'll recognize. I teach online with those sites and at www.writingitreal.com.

In addition, the Learning Annex (www.learningannex.com) has offerings in a number of cities. Its curriculum will give you access to classes with nationally known as well as local writers.

Many urban centers have renowned writing centers and smaller organizations that offer classes of interest:

> In the Washington DC contact The Writer's Center, 4508 Walsh Street, Bethesda, MD 20815, (301) 654-8664, postmaster@writer.org.
>
> In New York City, contact Gotham Writers' Workshop, 1841 Broadway, Suite 809 New York, NY 10023-7603, www.writingclasses.com, (212)WRITERS (974-8377) or (877)-WRITERS (974-8377) .
>
> In Boston, contact Grub Street Inc.,http://www.grub-street.org, 561 Windsor Street, Somerville, MA 02143, (617) 623-8100, info@grubstreet.org.
>
> In Seattle, contact Richard Hugo House, http://www. hugohouse.org, 1634 Eleventh Avenue, Seattle, WA 98122, (206) 322-7030, welcome@hugohouse.org.
>
> In San Diego, contact Silver Threads, www.silver-threads. org, 3830 Valley Center Drive, #705, PMB 102, San Diego, CA 92130, (858) 794-1597, info@silver-threads.org for information on memoir writing classes and editing help. Their

workbook, *Turning Your Life's Stories into a Literary Memoir* by Peggy Lang and Robert Goodman emphasizes their idea that well-dramatized theme and the hope of answering a burning question keep the readers' interest.

Wherever you live, don't hesitate to find out about writing classes by calling your arts council, bookstores, colleges and universities. Pay attention to the community ads in local newspapers and bulletin boards for announcements. If there are reading series in your area, the series sponsors are also a good source of information about classes.

Grants and Awards Listings

Poets and Writers carries a comprehensive listing of grants and awards online at www.pw.org/links_pages/Grants_ and_Awards and in its published quarterly. It is available by subscription and on newsstands.

Writer's Digest's *Writer's Market* has a good section on contests and awards.

The newsletters of arts commissions also notify the public about local and state grants and awards, as do national organizations for writers.

Online, visit www.wordsmithshoppe.com/writerscontests and www.winningwriters.com.

Listings of Writers Who Do Speaking and Teaching Engagements

Poets and Writers maintains a published directory.

The National Library of Congress has listings of writers.

Some states have writers-in-the-schools programs with listings. Visit www.writersintheschools.org/links.htm for links to many of them.

Don't forget to search by name on the Internet. Many writers maintain Websites that describe their services and fees and offer contact information. If you cannot locate contact information for a writer, you can contact their publisher who will forward your letter to the author.

Other Resources for Essay Writers

Book Review Publications

Booksense 76, *Bloomsbury Review*, the *Los Angeles Times Book Review*, the *New York Times Review of Books, Book Forum*, and *Book Magazine* are among my favorites. Reading them assures that you will know about new essay collections and have the pleasure each issue of reading essays about books. These magazines have online sites with subscription information. Type the name of the publication into the key word function of your search engine.

Respected Print Literary Journals

Reading periodic publications dedicated to the essay or creative non-fiction is one of the best resources for writing well. Subscribing to at least one per year and looking online for essays that appear in these journals is a good idea;choosing at least three—one national, one regional, and one local—and regularly browsing them is an even better idea. Browsing library and bookstore shelves for small press literary magazines with essays is a useful habit to develop. Reading the essays local, regional and national editors select helps you learn more about essays, and why and how they appeal to readers.

Here is a short list of journals dedicated to publishing essays. You can visit their websites for subscription information and writing samples:

Tiny Lights: www.tiny-lights.com, P.O. Box 928, Petaluma, CA 94953.

Fourth Genre: Explorations in Nonfiction: www.msupress. msu.edu/FourthGenre, Department of ATL, 229 Bessey Hall, Michigan State University, East Lansing, MI 48824.

Riverteeth, www.ashland.edu.colleges/arts_sci/english/riverteeth/ index2.htm Department of English, Ashland University, Ashland, OH 44805.

Creative Nonfiction, from the University of Pittsburgh, is available at reduced subscription rate at www.usubscribe.com.

The Georgia Review,www.uga.edu/garev, The University of Georgia Athens, GA 30602-9009, (800) 542-3481, garev@ uga.edu

The Bellingham Review, MS-9053 Western Washington University, Bellingham, WA 98225, www.ac.wwu.edu/~bhreview/ currentissue.htm

In addition to browsing the journals and reading about them online, you can also read about them in *Magazines for Libraries* at the reference desk of your local library. This reference has information about the origins, funding, leanings, literary status, and history of hundreds of journals.

Respected Online Literary Journals

Here is a short list of online journals with good reputations among the literary community. Visit their websites to read sample publications and for submission and subscription guidelines:

Brevity: Concise Literary Nonfiction: www.cnf.edu/brevity/ brevity13.htm

Drunken Boat: www.thedrunkenboat.com/

Salon.com: www.thedrunkenboat.com/

*Seven Seas Magazine:*www.sevenseasmagazine.com.

Some Anthologies You Might Enjoy:

McGraw-Hill's *Tell It Slant: Writing and Shaping Creative Non-Fiction* by Brenda Miller and Suzanne Paola has an anthology of over ninety essays.

W.W. Norton's *In Brief and In Short,* edited by Judith Kitchen and Mary Paumier Jones, are full and rich collections of very short creative nonfiction writing.

Penguin's *One Hundred Great Essays,* edited by Robert Diyanni is full of modern and contemporary essays. If you are intimidated by 100, you can buy the *Fifty Great Essays* edition; if that seems too big, there is the "starter kit" version, *Twenty-Five Great Essays* edition.

Houghton Mifflin's annual *The Best American Essays* is an anthology of yearly guest editor picks from among essays that appeared in magazines. Other similar annual anthologies include: *The Best American Sports Writing, The Best American Science Writing,* and *The Best American Travel Writing.*

Book Festivals

Los Angeles, San Francisco, Chicago, and Phoenix are among many cities that host book festivals either in the fall or spring. The festivals are often co-sponsored by the city's major newspaper. Big-name and local writers speak and offer panels and workshops. In addition, bookstores, publishers, distributors, and magazines among other organizations and companies rent booth space and promote writers and the written word. Becoming a member of the volunteer festival staff can help assure you a part in bringing writers to town and meeting them. See http://publishing.about.com/cs/bookfestivals/ and http://gailevans.tripod.com/gailevans/id24.html for a listing of festivals. Also, check the website of your local newspaper to see if they sponsor such a festival, or call your city or county arts commission.

Writing Groups

Whether you join a professionally facilitated writing group, a group that meets at a local bookstore or library, or form one by advertising in a local newspaper or library newsletter or contacting peers from a writing class, these groups can work very well. Meeting times provide deadlines, and the meetings provide an audience. An effective group supports works-in-progress and revision and shares information about publication, lectures, and readings of interest.

Since a team is usually more powerful than its parts, you can foster knowledge of essay writing and publishing by finding or establishing a group that is right for you. Chicago Review Press' *The Writing Group Book: Creating and Sustaining a Successful Writing Group* by Lisa Rosenthal includes more than 30 members of writing groups explaining how and why they found a group to join or established their own, how they helped their group flourish, and what belonging to the group helped them accomplish.

There are even online writing groups. To learn more about one such online possibility visit www.writers.com/groups.htm. In addition, Rosenthal's book has a section on online writers groups.

You can jump in almost anywhere and learn more about the writing life. Whether you start by reading how-to literature, going to conferences or classes, or just submitting your work, you are bound to attract information and opportunities. Keep your eyes and ears open, visit the bookstores and newsstands near you, go to author readings at bookstores, festivals, and civic events, and keep your connection to an online search engine up and running, Before long, your list of resources will include all you need to know. But never forget: the resources are supplements to the most important action you can take: Write your essays!

Contributors

James Bertolino has had nine volumes and twelve chapbooks of his poetry published, including *Pocket Animals* from Egress Studio Press and *Greatest Hits: 1965-2000* from Pudding House Publications. He has won book publication awards from the Quarterly Review of Literature Poetry Series for *First Credo* and *Snail River.* His books *Making Space For Our Living* and *Precinct Kali & The Gertrude Spicer Story,* originally published by Copper Canyon Press and New Rivers Press, have been reprinted online by the Contemporary American Poetry Archive at Connecticut College. He teaches poetry, fiction and creative non-fiction writing at Western Washington University and lives beside a mountain lake outside Bellingham.

Susan Bono is a writing instructor, freelance writer and editor living in Petaluma, California. Her work appears in newspapers and anthologies, on the Internet, and is a regular feature of Word by Word on KRCB radio. She has published *Tiny Lights,* a journal of personal essay, since 1995, along with its online counterpart at www.tiny-lights.com.

Janice Eidus is a novelist, short story writer, and essayist who has twice won the O. Henry Prize for her short stories, as well as a Redbook Prize and a Pushcart Prize. The author of four highly acclaimed books—the story collections, *The Celibacy Club* and *Vito Loves Geraldine,* and the novels *Urban Bliss* and *Faithful Rebecca*—she teaches writing privately, as well as at writers' conferences around the country.

Marjorie Ford's latest publication appears in the anthology *Making Connections: Mother-Daughter Travel Adventures* edited by Wendy Knight (Seal Press). She has presented women's health information through fiction in *Loving True, Living True* (Warner) and *True to Life* (Emory University), which was honored by *Ms. Magazine* and *Mademoiselle.* She is currently at work on *Sin Eater,* an autobiographical book about healing the soul. She writes and practices psychotherapy in Tucson, Arizona.

Susan Hagen earned first place in a national essay contest with her personal essay, "Softball." Much of her writing has been inspired by her experiences of growing up in a small town and her subsequent tenure as a firefighter in rural Northern California. Susan is co-author of the book, *Women at Ground Zero: Stories of Courage and Compassion* (Penguin-Putnam), a collection of first-person stories told by female rescue workers who responded to the World Trade Center tragedy on September 11, 2001. She also teaches writing classes and is a motivational speaker.

Janis Jaquith's commentaries are heard on NPR-station WVTF in Roanoke, Virginia, and nationally on Public Radio International's "Marketplace." Her newspaper column appears in Charlottesville, Virginia's *Daily Progress. Birdseed Cookies: A Fractured Memoir* is a collection of her radio essays.

Timothy L. Johnson grew up on a farm in North Dakota and majored in agronomy at North Dakota State University. After service in the Peace Corps in Brazil, he worked as an agricultural extension agent in North Dakota for 14 years. He then earned a Master's degree at the University of Arizona, Tucson and worked with international training programs for a number of years. Although he maintains ties to the farm where he grew up, he currently resides in Tucson where among other things he dabbles in writing and photography.

Christi Killien has published six children's novels and numerous essays. She is also Sheila Bender's co-author in *Writing In a Convertible With the Top Down: A Unique Guide for Writers*. She lives in Suquamish, Washington and is currently working on a memoir.

Linda Kulp is a teacher, freelance writer, poet and author of a picture book, *Treasure in the Attic*. Her articles and poems have appeared in various magazines, including *Hopscotch, Boys' Quest, Children's Playmate, Instructor* and *Potato Hill Poetry*, and in anthologies, including *Me, Myself and I; Families; Dino Roars*; and *Eating Through the Day*. She lives in Frederick, MD.

Nancy Smiler Levinson is the author of some 24 books for young readers, including history, biography, and historical fiction. With a background in journalism (University of Minnesota), she also continues to write for newspapers and magazines and has published numerous articles, essays, and op-ed pieces in periodicals ranging from *American Heritage* to the *Los Angeles Times*. She lives in Los Angeles. Her essay resulted from writing *I Lift My Lamp: Emma Lazarus and the Statue of Liberty*, Lodestar Books, 1986.

Susan Luzader, co-author of *Conquering Pain* (Berkley 1997) has published articles and essays in *American Medical News, Southwest Art, Personal Journaling, Alaska Airlines Magazine, Arizona Highways*, and many other publications. A charter member of the Fabulous Women Writing Group in Tucson, Arizona, Luzader conducts writing workshops to help fellow writers build their confidence and skills.

Roy Nims lives in Bellingham, WA. His essay "The Locker Room" was written for his college Freshman Composition class at Shoreline Community College.

Bora Lee Reed lives in Berkeley, California with her husband, Wes, and their daughters, Kate and Anna. Anna is now 4 years old. Bora gratefully acknowledges her friends in InterVarsity Christian Fellowship and Church without Walls, Berkeley, for their care during a time of great sorrow.

Joanne Rocklin, Ph.D. has written over 20 books for children, encompassing several genres. She has a doctorate in psychology and is a former elementary school teacher, presently writing children's books full-time. Both of her middle grade novels, *For YOUR Eyes Only!* (Scholastic) and *Strudel Stories* (Delacorte/Random House) were School Library Journal Best Books of the Year. *Strudel Stories* was named an American Library Association Notable Book. Her latest book is a beginning reader, *This Book is Haunted.* a HarperCollins I Can Read. Joanne teaches a class in writing children's books at UCLA Extension and gives frequent presentations in schools and libraries. She lives in Los Angeles with her husband Gerry, two cats, and one golden retriever.

Barbara Stahura is a freelance writer and editor in Tucson, Arizona. Her articles, essays, and poems have appeared in a wide variety of print and online publications, including *The Christian Science Monitor, The Progressive, Spirituality & Health, Science of Mind, Southern Indiana Review,* and MSNBC.com. She is a member of the Project Purpose Writing Team, a group of freelance writers who write and publish articles about people and institutions whose lives and missions are dedicated to a bold and inspired purpose. Her Web site is http://www.clariticom.com.

Sam Turner was born in Holbrook, AZ. He grew up on the South Rim of the Grand Canyon where he and Phyllis Jane Slocum were married June 16, 1957. Today, they teach astronomy and writing and are freelance writers living in Tucson, AZ.

Steven Winn has published personal essays in the *Baltimore Sun, Buffalo News, California Lawyer, Clackamas Literary Review, Cleveland Plain Dealer, Detroit News, Fort Lauderdale News, Good Housekeeping, Parenting, Parents, Seattle Times*, and *Seattle Weekly*. He is the arts and culture critic of the *San Francisco Chronicle* and winner of a 2002 Excellence in Writing Award from the American Association of Sunday and Feature Editors.

About the Author

Sheila Bender is a poet, essayist, book author and publisher of *Writing It Real*, (www.writingitreal.com) an online instructional magazine for those who write from personal experience. She holds a Masters of Arts in Creative Writing from the University of Washington and a Masters of Arts in Teaching from Keane College in New Jersey. She has helped hundreds of students begin to write, continue to write, and publish. In her books, online workshops, and texts on writing, she combines over two decades of teaching and writing experience with cutting edge exercises and encouraging step-by-step discussions.

She has written for *The Seattle Times*, *The World*, and *Poet Lore*, among other publications and has served as a columnist and feature writer on writing personal essays, journaling, and writing poetry for *Writer's Digest*. Her many books on writing include *Keeping a Journal You Love, Writing Personal Essays: How to Shape Your Life Experiences for the Page, A Year in the Life: Journaling for Self-Discovery*, and *Writing Personal Poetry: Creating Poems from Life Experience*. She co-authored *Writing in a New Convertible with the Top Down*. In addition to her instructional writing, Sheila teaches at writers' conferences and workshops around the country and online.

For more information visit her websites at www.writingitreal.com and www.sheilabender.com.